SERVICE QUALITY

A Profit Strategy for Financial Institutions

SERVICE QUALITY

A Profit Strategy for
Financial Institutions

Leonard L. Berry
David R. Bennett
Carter W. Brown

DOW JONES-IRWIN
Homewood, Illinois 60430

Figure 1-1, page 10, and the quote appearing on page 14 are reprinted with permission of The Free Press, a Division of Macmillan, Inc. from *The Pims Principles: Linking Strategy to Performance* by Robert D. Buzzell and Bradley T. Gale. Copyright © 1987 by The Free Press.

The quote appearing on page 87 is from *The Winning Performance: How America's High Growth Midsize Companies Succeed*, by Donald K. Clifford, Jr. and Richard E. Cavanagh. Copyright © 1985 by Donald K. Clifford, Jr. and Richard E. Cavanagh. Reprinted by permission of Bantam Books. All Rights Reserved.

Sponsoring editor: Jim Childs
Project editor: Jean Roberts
Production manager: Irene H. Sotiroff
Production services: Caliber Design Planning, Inc.
Jacket design: Renee Klyczek Nordstrom
Compositor: Eastern Graphics
Typeface: 11/13 Century Schoolbook
Printer: Arcata Graphics/Kingsport

Library of Congress Cataloging-in-Publication Data

Berry, Leonard L., 1942-
    Service quality : a profit strategy for financial institutions /
Leonard L. Berry, David R. Bennett, Carter W. Brown.
        p.   cm
    Includes index.
    ISBN 1-55623-094-X
    1. Banks and banking—Customer services.   2. Customer service.
I. Bennett, David R.   II. Brown, Carter W.   III. Title.
HG1616.C87B47   1988
332.1′068′8—dc19   88–19203
                                                                    CIP

Printed in the United States of America

    3 4 5 6 7 8 9 0 K 5 4 3 2 1 0 9

PREFACE

Wells Fargo Bank advertises a 24-hour telephone service line for checking customers. **First Union Bank** offers a money-back customer satisfaction guarantee on new personal checking accounts. **American Express** focuses its national advertising on its ability to help its members get out of difficult spots—both financial and nonfinancial.

Why are progressive organizations like these putting the spotlight on service? Because service is emerging as today's winning profit strategy for financial institutions. Bank analyst J. Richard Fredericks of Montgomery Securities describes this as an era of "Darwinian Banking," in which only the fittest institutions will survive. We agree and believe that fitness is a function primarily of two types of quality—quality of the balance sheet and quality of service. We leave to other authors books on the former subject. In these pages, we bring you our book on the latter subject.

Quality of service is a preeminent issue for financial institutions in today's intensely competitive, deregulated, narrow-spread market. It is the one strategy focus that is both important to customers and difficult for competitors to duplicate; it is the one strategy focus that offers simultaneously the potential for institutional distinctiveness and cost efficiencies.

Service Quality: A Profit Strategy for Financial Institutions describes the benefits, tribulations, and steps in developing service quality cultures in financial institutions. And it does so in part by letting service leaders tell their own stories. People like:

- **Security Pacific National Bank** Senior Vice President and Manager of Customer Service Administration Richard Davis, whose commitment to quality and expertise in branch management combine to make him the embodiment of the "service driver" we describe in Chapter 7.
- **Perpetual Savings Bank** Vice President of Training and Development Gail George, whose insight early on that service quality was far more than just another training issue enabled her to enlist the involvement of key line executives and pioneer a series of bank-wide service initiatives.
- **The Royal Bank of Canada's** Quality of Service Manager Keith Oosthoek, a savvy service leader whose enthusiasm and diplomacy have helped secure the commitment of diverse operating units to better serve both internal and external customers.
- **First American Corporation** Executive Vice President of Operations and Information Systems Willis Rhodes, who has applied a production and systems background to the management of bank operations. In building a "performance management system," he utilizes a shrewd understanding of how important it is to change the mindset of banking staff to achieve commitment to quality.

Service Quality: A Profit Strategy for Financial Institutions is for those senior financial institution executives who realize that their institution must improve service quality—and do it now. It's for those managers who want to get a service quality initiative approved, make it work, and keep it going. It's for every manager and nonmanager alike who has an inner sense of the importance of service quality, and who aspires to be a service champion in his or her own area. Our focus is on depository institutions—commercial and savings banks, savings and loan associations, credit unions—but we believe executives in other financial service sectors will find much that is relevant in these pages.

In this book, we bring together the results of a multiyear research program on service quality, our combined 40 plus years of working with many of the leading financial institutions in America, the existing published literature on service quality, and the practical advice and insights of dozens of service industry executives who we interviewed or surveyed.

This is a book of ideas, prescriptions, challenges. It is full of examples, stories, and verbatim quotations to illustrate our points, to bring them to life, to make them real. We have done our best to write a lively and readable book, a book that is serious but not boring.

The primary metaphor of the book is the service quality journey. Quality is not a "program." The job of quality is never completed; there is no destination. The service quality journey is littered with obstacles, and the unconverted are likely lurking in offices nearby and facilities distant. But the benefits of service excellence are profound. And they multiply as the journey continues.

We first heard the phrase "Quality is a journey, not a destination" in a 1983 American Marketing Association speech by Mary Rudie of Merrill Lynch. It was one of those perfect phrases that pop up intermittently, without advance warning, and powerfully capture the soul of a complex message. We use other metaphors in the book that we created, but credit for the "journey" metaphor goes to Ms. Rudie.

The first third of the book lays out the case for quality, provides a definitional framework for understanding quality, and discusses the gaps that cause service shortfalls. The last two-thirds of the book provide guidance for the service quality journey, from assuming a mantle of leadership to building a research program to organizing for service quality to formally recognizing service achievement.

Time is running out in the battle for the financial services customer. Everyone—or so it seems—is after everyone else's best customers. In writing this book, it has been our intent to describe the attributes of service quality from the customer's viewpoint and to provide practical approaches for taking action to improve the quality of that service. If, after reading this book, you are convinced that service excellence is critical to the profit performance of your institution, that service quality is a definable, understandable concept that you can "grab hold of," that many ideas and guidelines are available to you in assuming a mantle of service leadership, and that you, regardless of your current position, *can* make a difference in the service performance of your institution—then we will have done the job we set out to do. And, more importantly, you will be ready to embark on a journey that will favorably impact the long-term profitability of your organization.

Service Quality is a Profit Strategy!

College Station, Texas
San Francisco, California

Leonard L. Berry
David R. Bennett
Carter W. Brown

May 1988

ACKNOWLEDGMENTS

As with most projects of this magnitude, we owe a debt of gratitude to many people. The service quality research program that is the basis for much of the material in Chapters 2, 3, and 6 is a collaboration of Leonard L. Berry and A. Parasuraman of Texas A & M University and Valarie Zeithaml of Duke University. Sponsored by the Marketing Science Institute, the third phase of this multiyear research program is nearing completion as this book goes to press. Although Professors Parasuraman and Zeithaml are not authors of this book, their excellence as thinkers and researchers and their personal commitment to service quality have clearly contributed to the book's richness. For this and for their willingness to allow one member of the team to share the team's research with a financial services audience for which he has written for 20 years, we express our heartfelt thanks.

The service leaders profiled in Chapter 4 are especially appreciated for their insights and the example they set: Randall's Food and Drugs Chairman Robert Onstead; Crate & Barrel founders Gordon and Carole Segal; Southwest Airlines Chairman Herbert D. Kelleher; and Park Hyatt Hotel General Manager Paul Limbert. There are no finer service leaders anywhere than these individuals. A special thank you also to Colleen Barrett, Vice President Administration and Corporate Secretary for Southwest Airlines, who pulled together for us an incredible mountain of material on what is surely America's most fascinating airline.

Several individuals deeply committed to service quality at their own institutions also deserve special mention. These people contributed insights gained from first-hand service quality experience, and were instrumental in helping us develop the "real world" perspective of this book: Security Pacific National Bank Senior Vice President and Manager of Customer Service Administration Richard Davis; National Bank of Detroit Senior Vice President Robert DiAlexandris; Perpetual Savings Bank Vice President of Training and Development Gail George; Bank of Boston Department Executive-Massachusetts Banking, D. Bruce Wheeler; The Royal Bank of Canada Quality of Service Manager Keith Oosthoek; First American Corporation Executive Vice President of Operations and Information Systems Willis Rhodes; and McCormack & Dodge Director of Quality Resource Services Patrick L. Townsend.

Our research on the state of service quality today depended in large part on the cooperation of the individuals below, who gave freely of their valuable time to be interviewed or complete our surveys. The knowledge, candor, and enthusiasm with which these professionals supported our service quality research was invaluable, and we thank each of them for their personal contribution to this book:

Mason G. Alexander, Executive Vice President & Retail Banking Group Manager, 1st Federal of South Carolina

Lawrence Avril, Chairman and Chief Executive Officer, Hinsdale Federal Savings & Loan Association

Nick Baker, former Executive Vice President, Security Pacific National Bank

Joe M. Bailey, President and Chief Executive Officer, First RepublicBank Houston

Terry D. Bailey, Vice President, First Security Bank of Utah

Richard L. Barkhurst, Executive Vice President, First Interstate Bank of California

S. Neill Beavers, Vice President Retail Banking, Union National Bank

John Becker, President, First Wisconsin National Bank of Milwaukee

Kathryn E. Begley, Vice President, Corporate Public Affairs; Trustcorp, Inc.

Alexander Berry, III, Senior Executive Vice President, Signet Bank/Virginia

Cristy J. Blake, Marketing Officer, Corporate Bank Marketing; Norwest Banks

Thomas M. Bloch, President - Tax Operations Division, H & R Block, Inc.

Melanie L. Brammer, Quality Assurance Coordinator, Society Bank

Smith W. Brookhart, III, President and Chief Executive Officer, Centerre Bank of Branson

Russ Browne, 1st Vice President and Director of Marketing Services Division, National Bank of Detroit

Robert B. Bulla, President and Chief Executive Officer, Blue Cross and Blue Shield of Arizona

Leslie R. Butler, Senior Executive Vice President and Chief Administrative Officer, First Pennsylvania Bank

Patsy B. Cagle, Vice President, Louisiana National Bank

Stanley J. Calderon, President and Chief Executive Officer, Bank One, Lafayette

J. Harold Chandler, President, The Citizens and Southern National Bank of South Carolina

John Connolly, President and Chief Executive Officer, Constellation Bancorp

Norman Corzine, President and Chief Executive Officer, First National Bank

Timothy Creedon, former Executive Vice President, Valley National Bank

Thomas F. Crowley, Vice President Customer Service, Provident National Bank

Gerald M. Czarnecki, President, Honolulu Federal Savings & Loan Assoc.

James R. Daniel, President, Friendly Bank

John M. Davis, President and Chief Executive Officer, Fidelity State Bank of Garden City

Gus B. Denton, Executive Vice President, National Bank of Commerce

Mark A. Dinunzio, Executive Vice President Human Resources Group, First Interstate Bank of Arizona

Carole Dmytryshak, Senior Vice President, European American Bank

David R. Dowdle, Vice President, First Security Service Company

R. A. Duke, Jr., Assistant to the President, American National Bank & Trust Co.

Roland Dumas, Senior Director, Management Services; Omega, Consultants to Bank Management

H. E. Evans, Senior Vice President, Citicorp Diners Club, Inc.

William M. Fackler, Executive Vice President, Barnett Banks, Inc.

John Falzon, Senior Vice President Quality and Planning, Metropolitan Life Insurance Company

Meredith M. Fernstrom, Senior Vice President - Office of Public Responsibility, American Express Company

John F. Fisher, Senior Vice President, Banc One Corporation

Gary Foss, Senior Vice President and Director of Human Resources, Maryland National Financial Corporation

Susan H. Fowler, Senior Vice President, Sanwa Bank California

Gail George, Vice President of Training and Development, Perpetual Savings Bank

John D. Gilbert, Jr., Senior Vice President, First American National Bank

Thomas F. Gillett, Director - Network Service Planning, GTE Corporation

Ronald D. Glosser, President, National City Bank

Nancy Graham, Manager of Service Quality, Bank of America

John H. Hamby, Jr., President, Glastonbury Bank & Trust

Beverly Haddon, Executive Vice President, United Bank of Denver

H. Jim Harrold, former Vice President of Sales and Service, Canadian Imperial Bank of Commerce

Curtis M. Hastings, Jr., First Vice President, First Security National Bank & Trust

John E. Higgins, Jr., Senior Vice President, First Pennsylvania Bank

Gary E. Hoover, Chairman and Chief Executive Officer, Bookstop, Inc.

Jack Hull, Executive Vice President, National Director of Marketing; Coldwell Banker Residential Sales

Mark E. Huntley, Vice President - Sales Development, Meredian Bancorp, Inc.

Charles H. Jones, Jr., President and Chief Operating Officer, Gem Savings Association

John Keilly, Manager Marketing Strategy, Marketing Staff; Ford Motor Company

Thomas Kerstetter, Executive Vice President, Wilmington Savings Fund Society

Steven E. Kocen, First Vice President/Director of Marketing, First Security National Bank & Trust Co.

Jack Koehler, Service Quality Manager, Bank of America

Jack Kopec, Executive Vice President, Wells Fargo Bank

Ronald L. Koprowski, Vice President, Chase Manhattan Bank

William J. LaBelle, Executive Vice President and Chief Financial Officer, Mitsui Manufacturers Bank

Virginia LaGrossa, Senior Director, Omega, Consultants to Bank Management

Michel Larrouilh, President and Chief Executive Officer, Bank of the West

John P. LaWare, Chairman, Shawmut Bank

C. J. Lendrum, Deputy Director, U. K. Retail Services; Barclays Bank (London)

Obie L. LeFlore, Jr., Vice President, Continental Illinois National Bank & Trust

F. Harlan Loffman, Executive Vice President Retail Banking & Trust Group, First Interstate Bank of Arizona

Donald S. Lundy, Executive Vice President, SouthTrust Bank of Alabama

Robert G. Marbut, President and Chief Executive Officer, Harte-Hanks Communications, Inc.

Leslie E. Mathieu, Director of Sales & Marketing, The Bostonian Hotel at Faneuil Hall - Marketplace

Gary McCuen, Vice President and Manager of Corporate Service Quality, Bank of America

John A. Myers, Executive Vice President, Western Canada Individual Bank; Canadian Imperial Bank of Commerce

Michael Jay Moser, Assistant Vice President and Manager Marketing, The Idaho First National Bank

Bill F. Nash, Executive Vice President, 1st National Bank of Ohio

Robert L. Nellson, Senior Vice President, Fleet National Bank

William C. Nelson, President, Boatmen's National Bank

Peter R. Osenar, Group Executive Vice President - Retail Banking, AmeriTrust Co.

Norwood W. Pope, Senior Vice President Marketing, Valley National Bank of Arizona

Mary Jo Potter, Executive Vice President, Consulting Services; Omega, Consultants to Bank Management

George A. Rieder, Principal, George A. Rieder Associates, Inc.

W. Brent Robinson, Executive Vice President, American Savings

Richard M. Rosenberg, Vice Chairman of the Board of Directors, Bank of America

Donald G. Ross, Senior Vice President, Director of Customer Sales; St. Paul Federal Bank for Savings

John H. Rowley, Vice President and Division Manager, Atlantic Financial West Virginia

John D. Sasiadek, Director of Operations, MCorp, MBanks

Philip G. Satre, President and Chief Executive Officer, Harrah's Hotels & Casinos

G. Lynn Shostack, Chairman and President, Joyce International, Inc.

Raymond E. Skelton, Senior Vice President, Indiana National Bank

Gary F. Smith, Senior Vice President, Citizens Commercial & Savings Bank

Richard W. Spears, Senior Vice President, Indiana National Bank

Dan S. Spencer, Jr., Vice Chairman, United Missouri Bank of Kansas City

John A. Stacey, Senior Vice President, The Riggs National Bank of Washington, D.C.

Walter Stoewe, Manager of Corporate Planning, Home Federal Savings & Loan Association

Michael P. Sullivan, President, Michael P. Sullivan Associates

Fred Thiemann, Director of Measurement Systems; Omega, Consultants to Bank Management

Michael N. Trigg, Senior Vice President, Society Corporation

Donald F. Tuline, President and Chief Executive Officer, Richmond Savings Credit Union

Ann van Oppen, Controller, Omega, Consultants to Bank Management

Thomas C. Vick, Senior Vice President, First American Corporation

Allen J. Volkenant, Executive Vice President - Marketing, KeyCorp

O. Beech Watson, III, Vice President - Manager Sales Support & Training, Dominion Bankshares Corporation

D. Bruce Wheeler, Department Executive-Massachusetts Banking, Bank of Boston

Marcia Woodbury, Assistant Vice President - San Diego Division Customer Service Manager, First Interstate Bank of California

Michael Young, Assistant Vice President/Program Manager Training & Development, Valley National Bank

We extend special thanks also to Jim Childs, our sponsoring editor at Dow Jones-Irwin, who sat with us when we first planned the book, who read every word in the manuscript and made valuable suggestions, who developed the book's marketing plan and who, in general, did the things an editor should do with grace and skill. Jim Childs served us excellently and, in the process, he became our friend.

We also worked closely with Gene Crofts of Caliber Design Planning, Inc. during the production of our book and are appreciative of his diligence, care, and responsiveness.

And finally, last but certainly not least, a big thank you to Nancy Berry, who learned to use the Macintosh computer to type the final manuscript and who, pleasantly but firmly, would occasionally urge her husband to try again on certain sentences and phrases.

CONTENTS

Carlin Story.   Think High Tech, Not Just High Touch.
Service Quality Is a Design Issue.

SERVICE QUALITY

A Profit Strategy for Financial Institutions

PART 1

SERVICE QUALITY— THE ESSENTIAL CHALLENGE

CHAPTER 1

THE SERVICE
QUALITY IMPERATIVE

---

*The dollar bills the customer gets from the tellers in four banks
are the same; what is different are the tellers.*

—Stanley Marcus

Thomas Bloch, President of the Tax Operations Division of H &
R Block, tells the following story:

> A few years ago, a tax preparer in our company prepared a
> return for a woman who was deaf. Since it was cumbersome to
> complete the interview process as notes were passed back and
> forth between preparer and customer, the preparer was not
> satisfied with the thoroughness of the interview. That summer
> the preparer learned sign language so she could better assist the
> client the following year. The client returned and was impressed
> and grateful that the preparer cared so much to learn the new
> skill for her benefit. The client recommended the preparer to
> her friends who were also deaf. Today that same preparer has a
> large following of clients who are deaf, which has certainly ben-
> efited everyone—the clients, the preparer, and H & R Block.

Bloch's story is one of many legendary service stories that
we have come across in our research for this book. As part of
our research, we surveyed several hundred service industry
executives within and outside the financial services sector.
Their comments are sprinkled liberally throughout the book to
drive home not only the specific point of the moment, but also
the broader point that service quality is a "top of the agenda"
issue in the service sector today.

We begin with Thomas Bloch's story because it communicates powerfully that with service excellence, everyone wins. The customer wins. The employee wins. The company wins. The country wins. We agree with American Express' Executive Vice President for Operations Raymond Larkin when he states:[1]

> If U.S. companies in general are to continue to operate and grow, they need to exceed higher and higher hurdles of excellence. While this is particularly true in the world of banking and financial services where hundreds of new products and services are competing for the customer's pocketbook, it is equally true in the automobile business, the food business, or almost anywhere you look. People are smarter. More cosmopolitan. Consumer expectations, both yours and mine, are far greater now than they once were. Today's definition of high quality will be tomorrow's definition of minimum standard. This is the quality challenge that we, as a nation, must face.

Our theme is that service quality is a profit strategy for financial institutions. We have written this book to make the case for quality as a winning business strategy. Equally important is to provide in one package the research evidence, company experiences, and executive insights that show what must be done to build service-minded organizations.

We believe service excellence is the key strategic weapon for a service business! Our book is about service excellence for financial institutions—what service excellence is, why it is so important, what gets in the way, how to go after it. This book is written with a sense of urgency that we hope will be apparent to our readers.

SERVICE IS WHAT YOU ARE SELLING

Competing financial institutions are much alike in the services they offer—checking accounts, credit cards, individual retirement accounts, automobile loans. Their prices are comparative, and—with branch banking and automatic teller machines (ATMs)—they often offer comparable convenience of location. They may even look alike. Where they differ is in service. Competing institutions may offer the same services, but they do not offer the same service. Nobody knows this better than the customer. Quality of service is the great differentiator; quality of service gets—and keeps—the customer's attention.

The critical importance of differentiation is not lost on financial institutions today. By and large, their primary means of achieving it has been through market segmentation—identifying key target customer groups, then developing marketing mixes tailored to meet their needs. Although market segmentation does provide a basis for attracting a preferred customer base, it is very difficult to develop a stable of products that are distinct in the customer's mind from those offered by competing institutions pursuing the same market segment. Service quality can be extraordinarily important in achieving a distinctive offering.

"In our industry, it has always been difficult to distinguish one institution from another in terms of products and pricing," states Donald S. Lundy, Executive Vice President, SouthTrust Bank in Birmingham. "With the newer Demand Deposit Account and loan systems, products and pricing can be structured and introduced in a matter of days, or, in some cases, hours. 'First strike' capability will be in everyone's hands, but the competition can match whatever you do by the next morning. Product originality is important but short-lived. Is our senior management placing a priority on quality service? You bet we are! It remains the only real way a customer can differentiate between institutions."

Consumers agree that service makes an important difference. According to the 1987 *American Banker* consumer survey, quality of service is a major factor in winning customer loyalty. Survey results show that of the 10 percent of the public who moved their principal financial business to a new institution in the prior year, 21 percent did so because of issues related to service or errors. Only change of residence caused more people (25 percent) to take their financial business elsewhere.[2]

In addition, the people most likely to change financial institutions are affluent and between 25 and 40 years of age. Data collected by the MacGruder Agency, a marketing consulting firm in Aurora, Colorado, show that 75 percent of the people who close accounts for reasons other than a change of residence are middle and affluent market customers.

"We have far more people dealing with us as secondary bankers than we did before, and far fewer dealing with us as primary bankers. This is one of the costs we've had to experience because of poor service," comments a senior executive at one of North America's largest banks. "Our customers are no longer loyal to us. They leave us their basic banking needs, which we do very well, and take their auxiliary, high-margin business—consumer loans, mortgages, or retirement plans—to our competitors. Sometimes they go because of rates, but sometimes because of service. And they don't compare the other institution's service first. They left *us* because of service, and they'll go elsewhere just to punish us."

The message for financial institutions is clear: quality of service is a central issue. Good quality wins customers; poor quality loses customers. A close look at the financial services agenda for today and tomorrow reveals much that touches the service quality issue. As more and more financial institutions strive to develop internal sales cultures, their executives will see that sales and service are inseparable. As more institutions emphasize relationship banking as a way to do more business with existing customers for a longer period of time, their executives will see that service excellence is the surest way to keep their customers coming back.

One bank executive states emphatically, "We are in the service business! If quality deteriorates, so does revenue. In a commodity business like ours, the only thing that sets us apart is service."

SERVICE QUALITY IS A PROVEN PROFIT STRATEGY

The quality of service provided by a financial institution directly affects its bottom line. The effect will be positive if service is good and negative if service is poor, but the relationship between quality and financial performance is inescapable. As John G. Medlin, Jr., Chairman, President, and CEO of First

Wachovia Corporation, puts it, "Quality service is one of the few ways a financial institution can differentiate itself sufficiently in the marketplace to achieve exceptional business growth and earnings performance. It can help cut costs and boost revenues through relationship broadening, productivity enhancement, and error reduction. Therefore, service quality is a key element of our profit strategy."

The connection between quality and profitability has been well established by the Strategic Planning Institute through its Profit Impact of Market Strategies (PIMS) data base, which was established in 1972 to determine how key dimensions of strategy affect profitabilty and growth. Today, the PIMS data base contains financial and strategic information for approximately 3,000 business units. And according to PIMS research, quality counts.

In *The PIMS Principles*, Buzzell and Gale are unequivocal in claiming a relationship between profitability and relative perceived quality (quality from the customer's point of view).[3] They write, "Whether the profit measure is return on sales or return on investment, businesses with a superior product/service offering clearly outperform those with inferior quality."[4] Among the benefits that accrue to businesses offering superior perceived quality are the following:

- Stronger customer loyalty;
- More repeat business;
- Reduced vulnerability to price wars;
- Ability to command higher relative price without affecting market share;
- Lower marketing costs; and
- Growth in market share.

The PIMS data reveal that high relative market share combined with high relative quality exerts a strong positive influence on the profitability of a business. Firms that have both a higher market share and better perceived quality than their leading competitors earn returns that are dramatically higher than those of businesses with small share and inferior quality.[3]

Simple? Yes, as simple and logical as the fact that most

customers want good service and some of them will go elsewhere if they don't get it. That, however, is where it stops being simple. Although financial service executives admit the need for high quality service, they often view the obstacles in attaining it to be insurmountable—too many employees to reach, too many transactions every day, too many opportunities for something to go wrong. Just *defining* service quality is a challenge. That is why talk about improving service is more common than action among financial institutions, and why so few organizations today have formal, continuing improvement efforts.

But service quality improvement initiatives *can* work—even in huge, complex organizations like American Express—and they *do* have an impact on the bottom line. The American Express program was initiated in 1978 with three major objectives: (1) to maintain and build an established service reputation at a time when the company was doubling in size every three to four years; (2) to combat quality problems that were resulting in lost revenues and increased operating expenses; and (3) to show employees *how* to improve service. Since 1978, American Express has redefined service from the customer's perpective, set specific standards for service delivery, instituted a system to measure service performance worldwide on an ongoing basis, restructured organizational units and changed workflows to improve responsiveness and productivity, launched an extensive internal education and communications program, and established numerous reward and recognition programs around service quality. The bottom line impact of these changes —some of them wrenching and difficult—is impressive. To cite just one example, American Express claims to have added more than $70 million in revenue over a 10-year period by reducing cardmember application processing time by 50 percent.[1]

The evidence that service excellence pays off is strong and growing. From the massive PIMS data base to the many company case histories we encountered in researching this book to the anecdotes we gathered of single instances of exemplary service resulting in significant new business, the service performance/financial performance relationship is clear-cut. It boils down to differentiating the benefits of good service and the high costs of poor service. We now turn our attention to a fuller discussion of the costs of poor service—loss of market share, higher employee turnover, the costs of service errors, higher marketing costs, and lower prices.[5]

Loss of Market Share

Financial institutions have only three ways to increase market share: attracting new customers, doing more business with existing customers, and reducing customer loss. A reputation for poor service inhibits an institution's effectiveness in all three areas!

Research by Washington-based Technical Assistance Research Programs, Inc. (TARP) shows that a dissatisfied customer will tell 9 to 10 people about an unhappy experience—even more if the problem is serious—and will tell 5 people if a problem is handled to their satisfaction. Negative word-of-mouth not only discourages new customer prospects, but can impede cross-selling to existing customers, who will question doing additional business with an institution that offers faulty service. The TARP data also indicate that 31 percent of customers who experience service problems never register complaints because it is "too much trouble," there is no easy channel of communication, or because they believe that no one cares. Of that 31 percent, as few as 9 percent will do additional business with the company in question.[6]

If dissatisfied customers take their business somewhere else—and tell 10 people about their unhappy experience on the way—the inevitable result is a loss of market share and a corresponding negative impact on profits. The PIMS data not only establish the relationship between market share and profitability, but also between market share and quality, as shown in Figure 1–1. "The 1960s and 1970s brought a dawning realization that market share is key to a company's growth and profitability," write Buzzell and Gale. "The 1980s have shown just as clearly that one factor above all others—quality—drives market share. And when superior quality and large market share are both present, profitability is virtually guaranteed."[7]

FiGURE 1–1
Quality and Share Both Drive Profitability

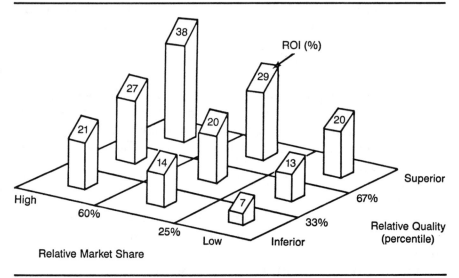

Source: Buzzell, Robert D., and Bradley T. Gale. *The PIMS Principles.* New York, NY: The Free Press, 1987, p. 109. Reprinted with permission.

It all goes back to the importance of differentiation among organizations offering a similar product mix. "We don't believe that cutting prices is an effective way to achieve profitable market growth," states John Becker, President, First Wisconsin National Bank of Milwaukee. "Consequently, we think the best way to differentiate ourselves in the marketplace is to offer a noticeably better level of service. When we talk about quality of service, we are referring to providing customers with service that consistently exceeds their expectations and requirements. Understanding customers' service priorities is an important emphasis."

Higher Employee Turnover

Another cost of poor quality is employee turnover. Just as high employee turnover can cause poor service, so can service problems lead to higher employee turnover. Operating policies that frustrate customers, overly long teller lines resulting from an emphasis on cost-cutting, and other such conditions can alienate good employees as much as they do customers, and cause good employees to leave. This can be a particularly pressing problem for financial institutions, where turnover among front-line service providers is already high because of low wages and limited advancement opportunities.

A senior bank executive claims that the biggest "roadblock" to service quality in his institution is the turnover and lack of experience of line employees. "This may be symptomatic of other problems, such as quality work space, inexperienced supervision, and difficulty in attracting staff to a central city location." If, in addition, line personnel continually face customers who are irate because of service problems beyond the employees' control, turnover is likely to be even more rapid.

Most service employees would prefer to be part of an "achievement culture" that challenges them to work to their potential and recognizes them when they do. Likewise, most service employees would rather give good service than bad service. As Raymond J. Larkin explains when listing the reasons why American Express inaugurated its quality assurance effort, "We were convinced that employees really wanted to do a first-rate job. If they were shown how to improve service, we knew they would be happier, prouder, more satisfied, and better workers."[8]

Institutions with policies and procedures that impede customer service—and without an internal culture that stresses employee satisfaction—face two service problems. First is the fact of high turnover itself, which creates an endless round of retraining employees whose tenure, in turn, is also likely to be brief. The second is the less than satisfied employees themselves.

Service firms that offer poor service are generally not fun places to work. Customers may be resentful, teamwork may be absent, supervision may be misdirected, recognition and rewards for superior effort may be nonexistent, and policies and procedures may be suffocating. Employees in a firm offering poor service are unlikely to recommend it to friends or acquaintances. It works the other way as well. Employees of a firm that stresses service quality will often "sell" others on the idea of coming to work for the company, which is one of the reasons why companies like Delta Airlines, Disney, and Nordstrom have so many applications for employment.

The Cost of Service Errors

Poor service steals from the bottom line. In a large institution, even an accuracy rate of 98 percent can mean hundreds of problems to fix tomorrow. One bank executive points out that "a lot has been written about the zero-defect programs in many companies, but my impression is that most employees still feel it is okay if they are right 90 to 95 percent of the time. This certainly does not help the customer who receives the inferior service."

Every mistake adds to the cost of the service delivery system, from extra computer time to fix account errors to adding more telephone lines and people to handle customer complaints. Audits at more than a dozen financial institutions show that the costs of poor service and ineffective customer communications add up to one-third of the total service workload.[6]

That estimate is echoed by Stanley J. Calderon, President and CEO of Bank One in Lafayette, Indiana, who states, "We believe nearly one-third of a typical financial institution's noninterest expenses are attributable to the absence of quality or the correction of errors and/or exceptions. By paying more attention to doing things right the first time and thereby making even modest improvements in error rates, significant cost reductions will result." Adds Obie LeFlore, Jr., Vice President of Continental Illinois Bank and Trust of Chicago, "Nonstandard item processing and adjustments are expensive costs."

American Express' Raymond Larkin believes that the most effective way of turning quality "nonbelievers" into "believers" is to quantify service improvements in terms of dollars and cents. He states:[9]

I can't emphasize enough that quality is as bottom line as a company can get. This is as true in a service business as it is in manufacturing. For example, in our Card business, there is re-work if errors are made in the first place—if remittances are not processed, if billings are incorrect, if establishments are not paid on time, if Cardmember benefits are not properly communi-cated. All this generates inquiries and additional processing—or what we call "avoidable input." Reducing avoidable input is the service equivalent to reducing rejects in manufacturing. It results not only in improved productivity, but also in happier customers, which translates into increased revenues.

Many financial institution executives spend the majority of their day resolving service problems. If a significantly in-creased number of transactions were done correctly the first time in error-prone institutions, executives would have the option of reducing staff substantially or focusing more staff time on sales or service extras. In addition, error-prone institu-tions have unhappy customers to contend with—customers who, if not handled properly, may become former customers. Thus, service errors are expensive not only because of the costs of correcting them, but also because of the potential for these errors to jar customer confidence. "We realize that the long-term costs of fixing the results of poor quality far exceed the upfront costs of acquiring/training the staff and obtaining/maintaining the resources necessary to provide high-quality service," says Peter R. Osenar, Group Executive Vice President, Retail Bank-ing for AmeriTrust Company. "We also know that delivery of consistently high-quality service attracts new customers—rec-ommended by someone who is already glad to call us 'their bank.'"

Higher Marketing Costs and Lower Prices

Inadequate service can lead to the toughest kind of marketing trap, namely, the need to increase marketing expenditures while simultaneously lowering the prices charged for products in order to compete. Indeed, it is not uncommon for institutions with poor service reputations to sustain market share losses even when they outspend their competitors on advertising.[5] On the other hand, positive word-of-mouth communications as a result of good service can allow a company to cut advertising costs. As Patrick McNarny, President of First National Bank of Logansport, Indiana, comments, "A good service reputation reduces the need for extensive advertising and thereby reduces advertising costs."

Likewise, relatively low prices frequently go hand-in-hand with poor service. The PIMS data show that companies noted for high relative quality are able to charge higher prices than their less service-oriented competitors. Buzzell and Gale write:[10]

> In the short run, superior quality yields increased profits via premium prices. As Frank Perdue, the well-known chicken grower, put it: "Customers will go out of their way to buy a superior product, and you can charge them a toll for the trip." Consistent with Perdue's theory, PIMS businesses that ranked in the top third on relative quality sold their products or services, on average, at prices 5 to 6 percent higher (relative to competition) than those in the bottom third.
>
> In the longer term, superior and/or improving relative quality is the more effective way for a business to grow. Quality leads to both market expansion and gains in market share. The resulting growth in volume means that a superior-quality competitor gains scale advantages over rivals. As a result, even when there are short-run costs connected with improving quality, over a period of time these costs are usually offset by scale economies. Evidence of this is the fact that, on average, businesses with superior-quality products have costs about equal to those of their leading competitors. As long as their selling prices are not out of line, they continue to grow while still earning superior profit margins.

For institutions with poor service, the combination of higher marketing costs and lower prices squeezes profitability which, in turn, creates a "Catch 22" situation—the company needs to invest to improve service, but management is in no mood to spend money because profits are so bad.

SERVICE QUALITY AND MARKETING

The differentiating benefits of good service and the costs of poor service make service-mindedness an imperative in an intensely competitive, deregulated financial services marketplace. The pivotal role for service is far from a mystery. The great service companies—from L. L. Bean to Federal Express—all compete on the basis of superior service. Competitors may match their lineup of services, outspend them in advertising, or undercut their prices, but matching their service commitment is tough. Service excellence springs from leadership and organizational culture—characteristics that cannot be purchased in a store.

L. L. Bean and Federal Express and many other legendary service companies use service quality as THE MARKETING WEAPON. Everything else revolves around service. In financial services marketing, it is no different. All of the key marketing initiatives depend on the delivery of first-rate service quality. We close the chapter with two cases in point—personal selling and relationship banking.

Selling Is Only Half the Story

Through the 1980s, one of the most dramatic changes in the financial services industry has been the growing emphasis on personal selling as a principal element in the marketing mix. Competition from nonbank companies with well-established retailing acumen; a proliferation of quickly copied, difficult to differentiate products; and the emergence of consumers who no longer regard financial institutions as merely a place to "park" their money have made personal selling and cross-selling skills essential. Selling, however, is only half the story.

Just as selling is essential in attracting new business, service is essential in keeping it. It makes little sense to invest heavily in commercial business or retail sales programs only to lose existing business through poor service. Attempts to build sales organizations with little attention to the service standards necessary to back them up often mean that existing customers are fleeing out the back door as rapidly as new ones are coming in the front. One of the respondents in our survey—the quality service manager of a major bank—makes the point in the following comment:

> Our bank, like many banks, has attempted to create a sales culture over the past several years. We recognized that we could no longer be passive and wait for clients to walk into the branch

and tell us what they wanted. In order to stay out in front, we would have to sell our products actively. We did that fairly well through sales campaigns, promotions, and loan officers who were cross-selling aggressively, but we weren't worrying about what was happening as a result of our service difficulties.

As fast as we were opening an account at the front counter, one of our tellers or customer service representatives would be closing an account at the back counter. We were selling wonderfully, but we weren't doing anything about keeping customers in-house. We've done some numeric studies on what we call "account turning," and it's amazing that many branches were richly rewarded for opening 600 accounts in a month, even though their actual position was only a net increase of 6 accounts.

Estimating that it takes about 25 minutes to open an account, the banker just quoted adds that the bank would have been far better off opening half the number of new accounts and using the extra time to provide better customer service. "We would have had a better chance to cross-sell more services, enhance the profitability of each relationship, and have a far more profitable bank."

Both selling *and* service are imperatives. Financial services organizations today cannot afford to be weak in either. Unfortunately, personal selling and service quality are often —and wrongly—viewed as opposites by managers and customer contact personnel. The following quotes from focus group interviews with bank employees illustrate the assumption that an aggressive sales posture requires sacrificing service quality:[11]

CUSTOMER SERVICE REPRESENTATIVE:

You are torn sometimes between giving customers what they want and bringing money into the bank. You know they can get a better deal elsewhere.

BRANCH MANAGER:

The teller's top priority should be taking care of the customer, and we have them out there selling.

TELLER:

> If I'm trying to cross-sell with a long line, the other customers waiting in line give me that look: "When is this girl going to shut up?"

CUSTOMER SERVICE REPRESENTATIVE:

> You don't focus on your customer. You focus on all these things you are supposed to sell. You have to do it, because the customer might be a "shopper."

In reality, selling and service are inseparable, particularly the kind of selling in which financial institutions engage. Financial services customers today are faced with a bewildering array of products keyed to specific markets, and similar in both nature and price to the product line offered by competing institutions. Selling these products requires personnel who can identify customer needs and sort through the institution's offering to propose just the right package.

In effect, good selling is part of good service. Helping customers to find just the right services to fulfill their needs—and doing so in an efficient and professional manner—is good service. It is only when service providers are asked by management to behave in ways inconsistent with customer desires that selling and service come into conflict. The problem suggested by the focus group quotes is not that sales and service are inherently conflicting, but rather that tellers are being asked to perform a different function than that desired by customers. That is the source of the conflict. Most customers want their tellers to be competent, swift, and courteous; they want their tellers to "move the line." In the customers' view, the teller window is for transactions, not selling. The new accounts and lending desks are quite another matter. These are sales desks and knowledgeable, need-directed cross-selling translates into good service.

Professional salesmanship is not slick hucksterism that leads people to buy products they don't need. On the contrary, professional salesmanship is helping customers make better decisions. Professional salesmanship at the sales desk is good service. And good service elsewhere in the organization supports salesmanship because it stems the loss of yesterday's "sold" customers.

Service Is Central to Relationship Banking

If sales and service go together, then they are also inseparable from the concept of relationship banking, the process of attracting, maintaining, and enhancing client relationships. True relationship banking involves the making of commitments— institution to client, client to institution. Service excellence paves the way to these relationships.

"Recently, the wife of an officer at another bank in our area called one of our banking offices for assistance in getting an 'on-us' check cashed," states one bank executive. "She was so impressed with the quality of service she received that she called our executive vice president at home and told him she was moving all her accounts to our bank!"

For the institution, the main benefits of building relationships are retention of clients and the opportunity to sell them additional services. Generally, it is more profitable to sell five services to one client than one service to five clients. The multiservice client is less likely to leave the institution entirely and easier to reach with a sixth service than is a new customer with the first service, and more efficient to serve on a cost-per-service-used basis.[12]

Since most aspiring relationship institutions are likely to face competitors with comparable products, pricing, and convenience, that takes us back to "well-serviced" as the competitive edge—and an approach to service that distinguishes between "client" and "customer":[13]

- Customers may be nameless to the institution; clients cannot be nameless.
- Customers are served as part of the mass; clients are served on an individual basis and handled with tender loving care.
- Customers are statistics. Their needs are reflected in

computer printout summaries. Clients are entities in and of themselves, and specifics about them—a demographic profile, a listing of services used, special requirements—are captured in a data base and then used to heighten their satisfaction levels.

- Customers are served by anyone who happens to be available; clients are served for their nonroutine needs by skilled professionals assigned to them—their personal banker, their personal problem solver.
- Customers have no particular reason to feel an allegiance to a given financial institution; clients perceive they have a personal relationship with the institution.
- Customers probably have a good reason to look for the best price or the best deal; clients have no reason to be "looking."

Most financial services marketers now recognize that marketing is about far more than attracting new customers to the institution. Most view "new customer marketing" as but the first step in the marketing cycle. Serving, selling, and reselling existing customers—and for those in selected segments, transforming customers into clients—this is seen as marketing, too. To these marketers, service is the organization's strongest opportunity for differentiation, the foundation on which other aspects of the relationship banking strategy rest. As H & R Block's Thomas Bloch states, "Our profit strategy is client-driven. Increasing profits is difficult to accomplish without increasing the repeat rate. Our repeat rate currently stands at 75.2 percent, and any changes in that rate are based to a large extent on client satisfaction."

SERVICE QUALITY IS A JOURNEY

The two routes to profit growth in financial organizations are cost-efficiency and differentiation. Excellent service quality contributes simultaneously to both of these objectives.

Service excellence fosters cost-efficiency. Every mistake adds cost to the service delivery system. Performing the service right the first time saves money directly by enhancing productivity, and indirectly by reducing customer loss. Many top executives at financial institutions recognize this fact, and are beginning to do something about it.

To achieve institutional differentiation, financial institutions need a strategy that is both important to customers and prospects and difficult for competitors to duplicate easily. Service is that kind of a strategy. The development of a strong service culture requires a multiyear, organization-wide effort that impacts the organization's fundamental mission and business strategy. Many factors are involved, including changes in the way goals are set, how performance is measured and rewarded, and the types of people who are hired.

Establishing a genuine service culture is not an easy thing to do. Because it is difficult, many organizations will not be successful in their efforts, and those that are will never finish the task completely. Service quality is a journey, not a destination. The journey never ends; quality is a continuous, day-after-day push to improve. It requires leaders throughout the organization who are obsessed with the idea of service excellence.

Service quality—like any journey—starts with a first step—a decision that the journey must be made. That initial decision must then be followed up by hundreds of other decisions, and those decisions repeated every day, day in and day out.

Fortunately, the road to service quality does not run through uncharted territory. Others are making the journey, and the evidence of its worthiness mounts. In our research for this book, we found that many financial institutions have begun the quality-of-service journey. Our purpose in this book is to help *you* find your way to increased profitability through service excellence.

We will follow the paths blazed by service leaders inside and outside of financial services to learn the lessons their experiences teach. We will examine the critical role of leadership in moving entire organizations along a new path. We will look at the many pitfalls and roadblocks along the journey, and discuss ways to avoid them. It is our goal to help you discover exactly where you are *now* along the road, and provide a roadmap that will help you get where you want to go.

NOTES

1. Larkin, Raymond J. "The History of Quality at American Express." *FYI.*, American Express Corporate Affairs, October 9, 1987, p. 5.
2. Gross, Laura. "Elite Customers Move the Most, Account-Switching Study Shows." *American Banker*, October 5, 1987.
3. Buzzell, Robert D., and Bradley T. Gale. *The PIMS Principles.* New York, NY: The Free Press, 1987, p. 107.
4. Ibid.
5. Berry, Leonard L. "The Costs of Poor Service Quality Are Higher than You Think." *American Banker*, June 24, 1987.
6. Goodman, John A., Ted Marra, and Liz Brigham. "Customer Service: Costly Nuisance or Low-Cost Profit Strategy?" *Journal of Retail Banking*, Fall 1986.
7. Buzzell, Robert D., and Bradley T. Gale. *The PIMS Principles.* New York, NY: The Free Press, 1987, p. 103
8. Larkin, Raymond J. "The History of Quality at American Express." *FYI.*, American Express Corporate Affairs, October 9, 1987, p. 2.
9. Ibid., p. 4.
10. Buzzell, Robert D., and Bradley T. Gale. *The PIMS Principles.* New York, NY: The Free Press, 1987, p. 7.
11. Berry, Leonard L. "Reconciling and Coordinating Selling and Service." *American Banker*, February 12, 1986.
12. Berry, Leonard L. "Financial Market Segmentation Can Be Powerful if Done Right." *American Banker*, October 10, 1984.
13. Donnelly, James H., Leonard L. Berry, and Thomas W. Thompson. *Marketing Financial Services—A Strategic Vision.* Homewood, IL: Dow Jones-Irwin, 1985, p. 113.

CHAPTER 2

TRUE SERVICE QUALITY—
THE FIVE ESSENTIALS

It's easy to look at financial services as an assembly line. Customers become just another product coming down the line, another bolt that needs a nut. But customers cannot be treated that way because each is different. We have to treat each customer as a customized product to which we add only the parts that are necessary.

—Customer service manager for a major
North American bank

If service is so profitable, why isn't it better? One reason is that the problem itself is a fairly recent development. The decline of service is seen as having begun in the inflationary 1970s, when prices rose 87 percent and consumers became willing to sacrifice service in their quest for lower prices. Self-service filling stations, off-price retail stores, and the spectacle of shoppers bagging their own groceries are at least partially the result of this tradeoff. Today, however, consumers realize they miss service. Although unwilling to give up many of the undeniable conveniences offered by technology—computerized systems for making hotel and travel reservations, for example—they still want personal interaction, particularly in situations where assistance is needed or there are problems to be solved.[1]

Likewise, the connection between service quality and profitability is new as well. Although Profit Impact of Market Strategies (PIMS) data have documented the relationship between market share and profitability for many years, it has only recently become apparent that quality is the one factor above all others that drives market share.[2]

Whatever the reasons, the service problem in American business and industry has started to attract a great deal of interest. A 1987 cover story in *Time* magazine states: "Personal service has become a maddeningly rare commodity in the American marketplace. Flight attendants, salesclerks, and bank tellers all seem to have become too scarce and too busy to give consumers much attention. Many other service workers are underpaid, untrained, and unmotivated for their jobs, to the chagrin of customers who look to them for help."[1]

In the financial services sector, executives sometimes throw up their hands in despair at the quality of service in their own institutions. One executive from a large midwestern bank recalls:

> Five years ago, after moving to a new job in a new city, I spent nearly 45 minutes with our own banking staff to set up a second account for my wife. Although I was a senior officer, the service was indifferent. Later the same week, I visited a Lord and Taylor store to purchase some clothing. Because I did not have checks as yet, I offered my MasterCard. The young sales clerk informed me that Lord and Taylor did not accept bank cards, but that she would be happy to issue a temporary Lord and Taylor card with a $350 limit, and could take care of it in minutes. In less than five minutes, I had my purchase *and* a new merchant relationship.

This executive is just one of many financial services executives across the country who realize the importance of quality service—its inescapable connection with selling and its value as a tool for building client relationships. Not all of them, however, have formal efforts in place to improve service. The challenge of truly upgrading service quality can appear impractical, if not impossible, and it is far easier to talk about the need to improve service than to really do it. Where do you start? Why are service-quality improvement efforts so difficult to implement? Part of the problem is the elusive nature of service itself. What is it, and what constitutes quality service?

WHAT IS SERVICE?

Before we can understand the concept of service quality, we first must understand the concept of service. By any definition, service is first a process. Whereas goods are objects, services are performances. Most observers agree that services have the following four characteristics:[3]

1. *Intangibility*—Services are intangible. In contrast to goods, they cannot be touched, tasted, smelled, or seen. Consumers who shop for services typically have nothing tangible to place in a shopping bag. Tangibles like plastic credit cards or paper checks may represent the service, but are not the service itself.

2. *Heterogeneity*—Services vary. Because they are performed—usually by human beings—services are difficult to standardize. Even the most courteous and competent tellers can have off days for any number of reasons, and inadvertently pass bad vibes or mistakes on to the customer.

3. *Inseparability of Production and Consumption*—A service is generally consumed while being performed, with the customer often involved in the process. A tasty restaurant meal can be spoiled by surly or slow service, and a routine financial transaction marred by long waiting lines or unknowledgeable personnel.

4. *Perishability*—Most services cannot be stored. If a service is not used when available, the service capacity is wasted.

These characteristics—especially the first three—pose quality challenges unique to services. The invisibility of services places a special burden on tangibles associated with them (for example, service facilities or the appearance of service personnel) to convey the proper "quality message." The labor-intensity of most services makes the pursuit of excellent service an ongoing adventure in even the best-managed companies. The inseparability of service production and consumption means the customer often visits the "service factory"—and experiences firsthand the good, the bad, and the ugly that may be present in this environment. In a goods manufacturing plant, production workers may have bad attitudes, language difficulties, or body odor and customers will never know. In a service factory—an airplane, a hospital, a branch bank—the bad attitudes, language difficulties, and body odor of workers are part of the customer's experience!

WHAT IS SERVICE QUALITY?

Only the customer can assess the quality of service, for quality, like beauty, is in the eye of the beholder. As Tom Peters points out, "the customer perceives service in his own terms. The customer alone pays the freight (or doesn't) for whatever reason or collection of reasons he or she chooses. Period. No debate. No contest."[4]

Attempts to improve service quality in financial institutions are complicated by the fact that bankers and consumers may define service differently. John M. Kolesar, President and CEO of American Trust Development Bank in Cleveland, states, "Bankers can't understand why consumers don't appreciate all the investment we've made in new technologies. . . . It's because they don't define 'service' as convenience. The new consumers' concept of service is far more qualitative. We need to bring our concept of service into line with theirs."[5]

Kolesar based his comments on a random sampling of Northeastern Ohio consumers who were asked to complete the statement, "I use my bank because it is . . ." from a multiple choice list. Eighty percent of the survey respondents chose "friendly" first. The second and third choices were "fair and respectful," and "convenient." A series of open-ended questions indicated that consumers think banking should be safe, quick, more caring, and courteous. They also felt their bank would be better if it: (1) "shortened waiting time," (2) "made fewer mistakes," and (3) "cashed checks with no hassles."

The Senior Vice President of Marketing for a major bank in the Southwest adds:

> If service to the customer is an operating ATM, a night drop, a short wait in a teller line, that is one thing. If it is a smile, a thank you, and a few personal comments about life in general, that is another. What constitutes good quality service for one person may not be important to another. Not everyone wants it

the same way. However, there are some basics that all service personnel must offer. These include product knowledge, courtesy, accuracy, and speed of transaction. We also find that quality is flavored by the environment, the cosmetics of the surroundings. Professionalism also ranks high in the perceived value of service; the attitude of the server makes all the difference in the world. In many cases, friendliness and genuineness overcome slowness or lack of great knowledge.

Quality service, then, is not "conformance to specifications," as it is sometimes defined, but rather conformance to the *customer's specifications*. There is a big difference between the former and latter perspectives. *Service organizations that do the wrong things for customers—no matter how skillfully they do them—are not delivering quality service.*

Service quality is both reality and perception—a chemistry of what actually transpires in the service encounter, and how the customer perceives what transpires based on preservice expectations. "Expectations" is a tricky word. It can mean what customers "think" will happen in a service situation, or it can mean what customers "desire" in a service situation. We are using the term to mean "desires." It is customers' service desires that shape their perceptions of an institution's service quality. Financial institutions achieve strong service quality reputations when they consistently meet—or exceed—customers' service desires.

And what is it that service customers desire? Berry, Parasuraman, and Zeithaml have investigated this question in research with retail banking, bank credit card, product repair, and long-distance telephone customers. From this research they have been able to identify five overall dimensions of service performance: tangibles, reliability, responsiveness, assurance, and empathy.[6,7] We now take a closer look at each of these dimensions of service performance.

Tangibles

Tangibles are the "seeable" part of the service offer—the facilities, equipment, and the appearance of contact personnel that provide physical cues to the nature of the service itself. Because services are performances rather than objects, they are difficult for customers to grasp mentally and impossible to grasp physically. Consequently, customers tend to look for tangibles associated with the service to help them judge the service.

One airline executive makes the point this way: "Look, if passengers notice a coffee stain on the flip-down tray when they get onto the plane, they almost automatically think that means you don't do your engine maintenance right."[4] The owner of a health and beauty spa adds: "It's important that I and the staff look fit, healthy, well groomed, and attractive —but not off-puttingly glamorous—because that is how our clients hope to look after our treatments. Would you go to a health and beauty farm with spotty beauticians and over-weight fitness instructors?"[8]

One way to convey an impression of quality service is to look like a quality operation. This means attention to details that seemingly matter little, but that when taken together, make an impression on customers, customer prospects, and employees. The first thing customers may notice when they enter the Friendly Bank in Oklahoma City is a floor so well-polished it can serve as a mirror. Customer prospects that tour the "backshop" operations facilities of National Bank of Detroit will likely notice the spotless check-processing equipment which is cleaned so thoroughly each day that its brass fittings almost shine.

Gerald Czarnecki, former President and CEO of Altus Bank in Mobile tells the following story about managing the tangible evidence:

> On a recent Saturday, an associate of mine happened by one of our off-site ATMs. To her dismay, she found the area an un-sightly mess, with receipt papers, deposit slips, Coca-Cola cans, and candy wrappers strewn about on the untrimmed grass. My associate took the sight personally; Altus Bank was not at its best. On her "day off," she stopped her car and policed the area. Since the job was only partially complete, she then drove home and returned with lawn mower, broom, and trash can!

Tangibles influence service quality perceptions in two ways. First, they offer clues about the nature and quality of the service itself. Friendly Bank's shiny floor and National Bank of Detroit's shiny equipment make one kind of statement, and a messy ATM site makes another. Second, tangibles can affect service quality perceptions directly. It is simply more pleasing to eat and work on an airline flip-down tray that is clean and not stained.

Reliability

Reliability involves performing the promised service dependably and accurately. In effect, reliability involves keeping the service promise!

Many of the organizations noted for excellent service have built their reputations on reliability. Federal Express earns its premium prices for overnight mail delivery by keeping its promise to get packages to their destination the next morning an extraordinarily high percentage of the time. McDonalds' customers consistently find the same product quality in Tuscaloosa as in Des Moines. And except for changes dictated by cultural preferences, McDonalds' customers will also find the same product quality in Stockholm or Paris.

As we saw in the last chapter, service errors are not only expensive to correct in a direct sense, they are also expensive indirectly, because they can jar the customer's confidence in the institution as a whole. Tom Peters quotes a Citibank officer assessing the loss of a potential billion dollar account, "We blew a $15,000 transaction. It was fairly early in a budding relationship. The client's response was 'If you guys can't get a $15,000 transaction right, why should I trust you with my account?'"[4]

Apologies are of limited value in rescuing unreliable service institutions. Most readers will identify with the anger present in the following story—anger stemming from broken service promises:

> Recently, I was turned away from an overbooked San Francisco hotel despite having a guaranteed reservation. A guaranteed hotel room represents an explicit service promise. The customer prepays for a room in exchange for the hotel's promise not

to sell it to anyone else. My biggest concern at the time was the people who would be telephoning me at the hotel. I was assured by the front desk staff that my calls would be forwarded to my new hotel, which was owned by the same company. This promise was broken also. The first hotel made two service promises to me and broke both of them. I shall never stay there again. I—as do many consumers—have a long memory.[9]

We advocate that financial institution executives place a premium on doing the service right the first time. Although the reality of 100 percent reliability is inherently elusive when human beings perform services, an attitude that prizes "zero defects" surely leads to an improved reliability percentage. For financial institutions, even a 98 percent reliability figure should not be considered acceptable. It may sound impressive, but what it really means is that 2 percent of the customers—a significant number in large institutions—are not receiving the service they were promised. An unhappy experience at a fast-food outlet is likely to mean that a customer's next burger will be made by a competitor. A mistake with something as important as people's money is even more likely to mean a lost customer.

Responsiveness

Responsiveness is readiness to serve; it is the willingness to serve customers promptly and efficiently. Financial institutions whose customers can't get through on busy phone lines —or that have long queues in the branches as a result of understaffed teller stations—are not likely to be perceived as responsive.

Employees at Home Depot, an Atlanta-based chain of home improvement warehouse stores, are taught to stop whatever they are doing when customers need service and either help them or take them to the right place for the appropriate service. This emphasis on being responsive to customers— communicated by a top management that participates personally in the training of staff prior to new store openings—is perhaps the principal reason Home Depot has been one of the fastest growing retailers in America during the 1980s.

When financial services executives relate favorite stories about customer service at their institutions, the responsiveness of individual personnel is frequently cited. F. Harlan Loffman, Executive Vice President, Retail Banking and Trust Group of First Interstate Bank of Arizona, tells the story of a recently widowed client who was a nonEnglish-speaking Mexican national:

> She and her husband had kept most of their monies in American banks, primarily with one of our major competitors. She had only a small account with us, and had never been in our Nogales branch before. Our customer-service representative, who spoke fluent Spanish, began conversing with her and soon found out that she was seeking advice about trust and estate services. She was not happy with the treatment she had received after first going to our competitor. The customer-service representative immediately phoned the Trust Division and put the client in contact with a knowledgeable trust officer who was also fluent in Spanish. Although the Trust Officer's office was 180 miles away, he agreed to a Saturday meeting in Nogales with the woman and her two sons, who were lawyers in Mexico. It was the first of several meetings, all on Saturday and all in Nogales. The woman was so pleased with our service and willingness to be of assistance that she opened her trust account with us, which turned out to be one of the largest individual trust accounts that we ever opened. I like this story not only because it demonstrates the value of quality customer service, but also the teamwork needed within the organization to be successful.

Responsiveness involves making it abundantly clear to customers that you want and appreciate their business. Like the other dimensions of service performance, responsiveness is often a function of "little things"—a branch manager unlocking the lobby door at 5:03 P.M. for an out-of-breath customer arriving just after closing time, a roving branch employee who makes sure that customers standing in teller lines are in the proper line and have their paperwork in good order.

Stew Leonard's, the much-heralded Connecticut food store, keeps at least 20 checkout lanes open at all times, keeps all of them open on the busy weekends, and passes out ice cream cones and other free goodies to waiting customers when checkout lines are especially long.

Assurance

Assurance refers to the courtesy and competence of service personnel that instill trust and confidence in customers. When customers deal with service providers who are both pleasant and knowledgeable, they are "reassured" about doing business with the right company. Courtesy without competence, or competence without courtesy, does not have the positive impact on customers that the combination of these characteristics can have. Finding these attributes of performance in the same service provider is no sure thing, as any service customer will attest.

The simple lack of courtesy is the most common characteristic of the service horror stories that are quickly becoming part of our popular culture. Comedian Jay Leno says that when he chided a supermarket clerk for not saying thank you, she snapped, "It's printed on the back of your receipt!"[10]

Other stories, fortunately, are more encouraging. Bank One's Stanley J. Calderon describes going to a branch office to give a "We Care Award" to an employee:

> We recently had some problems with our data processing, and I thanked her for her extraordinary efforts in dealing with our customers during this difficult period. I commented to her that it must be hard to always be friendly to people when you have so many problems with their statements. She looked at me quizzically and said she had no idea what I was talking about. She stated that treating customers well is the easiest thing she does —that it is actually harder for her to do otherwise and she doesn't understand why anyone would have difficulty delivering excellent customer service. After all, isn't that how we would want to be treated if we were the customer?

Making sure that common courtesy is more common is one challenge. Another is coupling knowledgeability with courtesy. The rapid proliferation of new financial products in the aftermath of deregulation has heightened the challenge. One researcher reports that in a simple test of financial product knowledge, bank customer-service representatives scored only 44 percent, compared to bank customers who scored 36 percent.[11]

Delivering on the assurance dimension of service performance requires careful selection of customer contact personnel and continuous training—topics that we will address later in this book. For now, suffice it to say that assurance results from putting the right people in the right environment and not from any sort of magic. When an executive of service-rich Nordstrom was asked how she gets new employees to understand the Nordstrom culture, she responded simply, "What we do is try to hire the best kids."

Empathy

Empathy goes beyond professional courtesy. It is commitment to the customer—the willingness to understand the customer's precise needs and find just the right answer to them. Empathy is caring, individualized, need-meeting service.

In service industries characterized increasingly by high technology—like financial services—empathy is an antidote, offering the countervailing "human touch" that can create genuine client relationships. "You can't get mad at an ATM unless it's closed or eats your card," says a Texas banker. "You don't expect more than you're going to get. But when you walk up to someone's desk, your expectations are higher. . . . You expect someone to understand what your problem is, to be concerned about it, and to show some willingness to try to cure it."

Smith W. Brookhart, III, President and CEO of Centerre Bank of Branson, Missouri, ties empathy into a package with assurance and responsiveness, and offers examples of how empathy can affect client relationships:

- The three widows in the nursing home who send the bank thank-you cards because a personal banker visits them.
- The lady who recently became a widow and comes into the bank every day because it is a place where she can get a hug from people who care about her.
- Older people who come in to ask for help in understanding the new financial products being advertised each day.

Brookhart adds, "Basically, we have found that when people who are seeking personal services trust us, the cost of the service is not a major concern. Clients perceive they are dealing with professionally competent people, and have a high level of confidence in these dealings. They have expectations of the service they want, and what they receive meets or exceeds these expectations. Bankers, in turn, must care about the client's needs and wants, and be willing to go beyond the last mile to get them achieved."

Empathy goes beyond the "Golden Rule." That people should provide the kind of service they, in turn, would like to receive is an inarguable "given" in any discussion of what constitutes quality service. Really caring about customers, making the effort to understand their needs, and finding a way to satisfy them constitutes the empathy dimension. When you have a customer who comes into the bank because she needs a hug, it is clear that some empathy is in the air.

The alert reader will note a close relationship between empathy and responsiveness. They are indeed closely related. It is helpful to think of responsiveness in terms of "access to the service," and empathy in terms of "understanding precisely the customer's service requirement." The institution that still closes its lobby at 3 P.M. jeopardizes its image of responsiveness. The institution that makes little effort to listen to customers jeopardizes its capacity for empathy.

SOME CONCLUSIONS ABOUT SERVICE QUALITY

Berry, Parasuraman, and Zeithaml asked their samples of retail banking, bank credit card, long-distance telephone, and product repair customers to rate the importance of the five service dimensions on a scale of 1 (not at all important) to 10 (extremely important).[6] Although all were considered to be important by respondents, the dimension of *reliability* ranked above all others as the single most important factor in judging service. This was true regardless of the specific service category being studied.

Customer expectations of service organizations are loud and clear: look good, be responsive, be reassuring through courtesy and competence, be empathetic but, most of all, be reliable. Do what you said you would do. Keep the service promise.[6]

Service quality is not the slippery, mystical, or amorphous concept it is often thought to be. Customers will give an institution high marks for its service when it meets or exceeds their service desires. The five dimensions of service performance give direction to the service quality journey. Although these dimensions will be differentially important to various market segments, on an overall basis, they all are important. As a group, they frame the essence of the service quality mandate: *to be excellent in service, seek to be excellent in tangibles, reliability, responsiveness, assurance, and empathy.*

In embarking on the service quality journey, it is well to keep the following perspectives in mind:

1. Improving service is very much a human enterprise. Three of the five service performance dimensions (responsiveness, assurance, and empathy) result directly from human performance, and a fourth (reliability) often depends on human performance. Even tangibles relate inasmuch as the physical appearance of service providers can influence service quality impressions. Clearly, the "people factor" is central to understanding what causes service problems, and what needs to be done to improve service.

2. The way customers judge a service may depend as much or even more on the service *process* than on the service *outcome*. In services, the "how" of service delivery is a key part of the service. Purchasers of tangible products judge quality on the basis of the finished product—its durability, functioning, appearance, and so on. Purchasers of services judge quality on the basis of experiences they have during the service process as well as what might occur afterwards. To financial services customers, a lending officer who is curt or intimidating during the

loan interview is a financial institution that is curt or intimidating.

3. Customers evaluate service quality at two different levels. One level is the "regular" service, for example, the routine distribution of the monthly statement. The second level is when a problem or exception occurs with the regular service, for example, when the monthly statement contains an error. Institutions that are great at problem resolution—that are highly responsive and reliable, reassuring and empathetic as well—are far more likely to repair any damage done by falling short on the regular service than are institutions that take a casual, "we'll get to it when we can" approach. Service customers are all too familiar with the hassles that can befall them in trying to get a service problem straightened out. Thus, they are likely to notice and remember when a service firm handles the problem-solving situation effectively. Financial services organizations that zealously pursue error-free service *and* that also gear up to respond effectively to those errors and problems that do occur will benefit from two powerful approaches to service quality improvement.

4. Everyone in a financial institution is a service provider; tellers, secretaries, check sorters, platform personnel, telephone operators, and auditors all perform some kind of service for someone else. Everyone in the organization has a customer, and each person's Number-1 priority day in and day out should be to meet or exceed that customer's service expectations. The internal services that "backshop" personnel perform are no less important in matters of service quality than the external services that "frontshop" personnel perform. Indeed, the quality of service delivered by customer contact personnel often depends on the quality of internal services delivered to them by operations personnel. As J. Harold Chandler, President of Citizens and Southern National Bank of South Carolina states, "Service quality incorporates a pride in company and self, as well as an attitude

of care for the customer. But service quality does not stop with branch personnel; it includes operations and others who have an indirect contact with our customers and with our own branch staff."

CLOSING THE SERVICE GAP

The service quality challenge boils down to closing the gap between the service that customers expect and the service that they perceive is delivered. It sounds so simple, but in fact, it is not simple at all. The good news is that service quality is definable and measurable. Service quality does have a handle that we can grab and hold. Without definition, the service quality journey is destined to be an aimless wandering in a desert of good intentions.

The bad news is that so much can get in the way of good service quality—even when we know what we are doing. The service quality journey is strewn with pitfalls, hazards, and obstacles, which are the subject of the next chapter.

NOTES

1. Koepp, Stephen. "Pul-eeze! Will Somebody Help Me? *Time*, February 2, 1987.
2. Buzzell, Robert D., and Bradley T. Gale. *The PIMS Principles.* New York, NY: The Free Press, 1987.
3. Zeithaml, Valarie A., A. Parasuraman, and Leonard L. Berry. "Problems and Strategies in Services Marketing." *Journal of Marketing*, Spring 1985.
4. Peters, Thomas J. "Common Courtesy: The Ultimate Barrier to Entry." *Santa Clara Magazine*, Summer 1984, p. 4.
5. " 'Service' Means Different Things to Bankers and Their Customers." *American Banker*, December 16, 1986, p. 6.
6. Berry, Leonard L., A. Parasuraman, and Valarie A. Zeithaml. "The Service-Quality Puzzle." *Business Horizons,* July–August 1988.
7. Parasuraman, A., Valarie A. Zeithaml, and Leonard L. Berry. "SERVQUAL: A Multiple-Item Scale for Measuring Consumer

Perceptions of Service Quality." *Journal of Retailing*, Spring 1988.

8. Rushton, Angela M., and David J. Carson. "The Marketing of Services: Managing the Intangibles." *European Journal of Marketing*, 1985, pp. 34–35.

9. Berry, Leonard L. "8 Keys to Top Service at Financial Institutions." *American Banker*, August 5, 1987, p. 4.

10. Koepp, Stephen. "Pul-eeze! Will Somebody Help Me?" *Time*, February 2, 1987, p. 50.

11. Stanley, Thomas O. "Inadequate Product Information." *The Bankers Magazine*, March–April 1984.

CHAPTER 3

WHAT GETS IN THE WAY
OF SERVICE QUALITY?

Getting a service quality improvement effort started in a big way and keeping it rolling is the major issue. Such a gigantic effort is required to overcome inertia that the size of the problem becomes its own roadblock. It is not just a matter of saying, "OK, people, let's smile and use the customer's name." Genuinely improving the quality of service is an everlasting effort. It's like switching from breathing air to breathing water.

—*John F. Fisher, Senior Vice President, Banc One Corporation*

Nobody sets out to give bad service. Yet service shortfalls occur with alarming frequency in organizations with the best intentions. In a 1984 *Wall Street Journal* article, "Service with a Smile? Not by a Mile," Jim Mitchell wrote, "The message of the commercials is 'We want you!' The message of the service is 'We want you unless we have to be creative or courteous or better than barely adequate. In that case, get lost!'"

Clearly, good service is central to the success of a service business. With what can service companies compete if not service? All of the truly successful service companies pay considerable attention to service quality; in these companies, service is viewed as a central, competitive weapon rather than a defensive measure peripheral to the main agenda of the business.

So what is the problem? What gets in the way of good service? Why is good service—which makes so much sense for service companies to provide—seemingly so hard for customers to find? The research team of Parasuraman, Zeithaml, and Berry has identified four overall gaps within service organizations that individually or in various combinations cause a fifth gap—a gap between customers' service desires and their perceptions of the service that is actually delivered. The four gaps that lead to service quality shortfalls are:[1]

Gap 1—Management's perceptions of customer service expectations are different from actual customer desires.

Gap 2—Management's specifications for service are different from its perceptions of customer expectations.

Gap 3—The service that is delivered is different from management's specifications for the service; and

Gap 4—What is said about the service in external company communications is different from the service that is delivered.

These gaps and their relationships are captured in the model shown in Figure 3–1. In this chapter, we discuss the nature and character of these service quality gaps in more detail.

GAP 1: THE DIFFERENCE BETWEEN WHAT CUSTOMERS WANT AND WHAT MANAGEMENT THINKS THEY WANT

When management fails to understand customer desires for the service, a chain reaction of mistakes is likely to follow. The wrong service standards. The wrong training. The wrong types of performance measurements. The wrong advertising. And so forth.

As stressed in the previous chapter, the customer's definition of service quality is the only definition that counts. Delivering superior quality of service starts with determining what customers want from the service; it starts with isolating the most important expectations of target markets. Determining the principal wants of targeted customer groups clarifies what must be done in the organization to satisfy these wants. It is tough enough to satisfy customer service desires without the added burden of not really knowing what desires to satisfy.

FIGURE 3-1
Service Quality Model

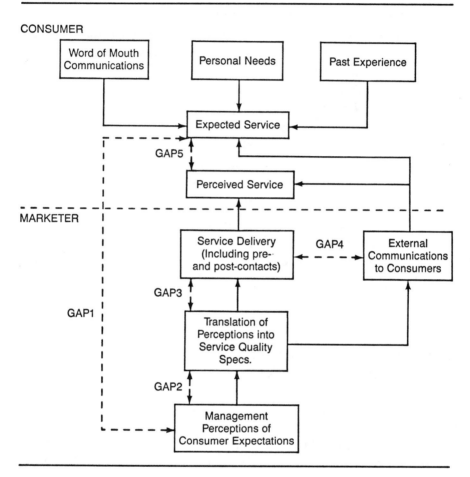

Source: A. Parasuraman, Valarie A. Zeithaml, and Leonard L. Berry. "A Conceptual Model of Service Quality and Its Implications for Future Research." *Journal of Marketing*, Fall 1985, pp. 41-50.

Gap 1 is such an obvious hazard that one could legitimately question why it would ever occur in financial institutions. But it does occur, and does so frequently. Why? One reason is that some senior executives believe they already know what their customers want and do not invest in formal marketing research to track customer desires. A complicating factor is that managers of financial institutions are very different from their customers. A majority of Americans earn less than $30,000 a year and have less than $8,000 in savings. Few senior managers fit this profile. The failure to do ongoing and appropriate research on customer service expectations results in wrong, imprecise, or incomplete management perceptions. Financial service customers are complex beings who differ from one another and who change over time (which is why the market is sometimes referred to as "a moving target"). It is sheer folly to ever believe that research is unnecessary for a clear, precise, and timely picture of customer service expectations.

Another factor that contributes to Gap 1 is when management spends too little time conferring directly with customers and employees in the field. Formal research—as valuable and necessary as it is—is no substitute for direct contact with customers and employees. The computer printout filled with research findings complements but does not replace face-to-face contact between management, customers, and employees. Computer printouts provide averages, summaries, and global pictures. Face-to-face encounters with customers and employees provide nuances, interpretive shadings, and tone. Customers can express their service desires and reactions with a forthrightness or depth of feeling that does not come through in formal research reports. Employees who have frequent contact with customers can add their perspective on customer service desires, as well as describe obstacles to better service performance in the organization.

A third factor that influences Gap 1 is the number of management levels between service personnel and top management. The more intermediaries there are between the service floor and the executive suite, the more difficult it can be for top management to get a clear picture of customer service expectations. Multiple middle management layers mean opportunities for filtering and distorting information needed by senior management. Also, organizational complexity and bigness can discourage top management from even trying to regularly communicate with frontline service providers and their customers. As one major bank executive explains, "Size inhibits face-to-face communications, makes the creation of a 'team' more difficult, and requires top management hustle to retain a 'high-touch' style. Size can foster an atmosphere of coolness."

GAP 2: THE DIFFERENCE BETWEEN WHAT MANAGEMENT BELIEVES CUSTOMERS WANT AND WHAT IT ASKS THE ORGANIZATION TO DELIVER

Management may understand customer service expectations, but not translate this understanding into equivalent specifications for service performance. Insufficient management commitment to service quality, a short-term profit orientation, perceived difficulty in establishing service standards and measurements, and the sense that it is simply not feasible to meet customer service desires all can lead to discrepancies between what management believes customers want and what it asks the organization to deliver.

Insufficient Management Commitment

Financial institution executives surveyed for this book agree that management commitment is the single most important factor in building a service-minded culture—and that the lack of it can be the biggest roadblock. As one bank president explains, "The corporate culture must support the quality perspective or service will deteriorate into mediocrity. If there is a breakdown anywhere in the organization, this drive to maintain quality cannot be maintained."

Insufficient management commitment to service quality allows undue emphasis on cost reduction and short-term profitability to prevail. One prominent banker is especially blunt in his assessment:

> The biggest roadblock to service quality in banks is numbers-driven management. Behind (management) are earnings-driven analysts. If bankers were given time to get their act together,

establish the appropriate program, provide the support it requires, and in time (perhaps three years later) show the results, without penalty in the interim, the culture might change. But few bankers have the time or resources to throw against such a nebulous thing as service quality, even if they knew what it was. So they just talk about it.

Other executives surveyed drew similar conclusions:

- "As net interest margins continue to decline, most line management people look to cut costs anywhere possible and increase individual productivity. Volumes tend to be more important than quality service."
- "One of our roadblocks is a predisposition to relate service quality improvement to higher costs in an environment where our cost factors already seem substantial."
- "Staffing for efficiency has made it nearly impossible for some employees to probe, question, counsel, and interact with customers on other than a cursory basis."
- "Employees mistake cost-containment as an excuse for lack of quality. Too many institutions do not take the time or spend the money to have well-trained, motivated employees at all levels who understand how their jobs affect the customer."
- "Unfortunately, we have concentrated so much on cost-containment that we have not given proper emphasis to removing roadblocks. In bureaucratic industries such as ours, these roadblocks become very difficult to remove."

As this string of quotes suggests, management preoccupied with cost-containment and short-term earnings is not likely to be enamored with the idea of raising service standards (or even articulating such standards), if to do so would add cost in the short-term. Ignored by managers preoccupied with short-term financial performance is the reality that investments to improve service not made in the short-run are therefore not made in the long-run either, since the latter is merely a culmination of units of the former. Also ignored is the fact that good service is not the same thing as "body counts." Alexander Berry, III, Senior Executive Vice President of Signet Bank/Virginia, claims that bankers who equate better service with "more people, more machines, and more space do not understand that service quality is 'heart,' not 'things.'"

Perceived Difficulty in Setting Service Standards

Another reason management may not translate customer service desires into service standards is that it views service quality as a mushy construct for which it is difficult, if not impossible, to set precise standards. The prospect of breaking down the service act into definable and measurable units of performance is daunting and often results in weak attempts to establish meaningful standards and measures. As one bank president states, "We have in the past measured only that which was easy to measure. Now we concern ourselves with the measurement and improvement of the service quality we provide. But the careful establishment of well-conceived personal goals . . . is still difficult for us."

Another banker adds, "Our lack of precise, ongoing service quality measurements hinders specific quality goal setting, leaves quality as a somewhat indeterminant factor in compensation decisions, and may not result in appropriate difficulty/results recognition."

What these comments suggest is that some managements do not know how to establish effective service standards and measures. They establish service standards that are too informal or general or otherwise off-target, not because they lack commitment to service quality, but because they find setting service standards a difficult endeavor. Many key questions arise, including: How many service standards are enough? How do you decide which standards are most important? How do you set standards for nonstandardized services, for example, commercial lending? How do you avoid conflicting standards?

In fact, setting service standards is not as imposing a challenge as it appears. The above questions are answerable, as we shall see later in the book. Nonetheless, perceptions shape behavior, and the common perception that service standards and measures are mushy, unscientific, and "soft" inhibits the closing of Gap 2.

Perceived Difficulty in Meeting
Customer Expectations

Gap 2 problems will also occur if management does not believe that meeting customer expectations is feasible. Parasuraman, Zeithaml, and Berry have written about service executives who, in interviews, cited constraints preventing them from delivering the level of service customers expected.[1] For example, executives in a repair service firm they studied knew that consistently fast response to service requests was important to customers. These executives considered such consistency to be a problem because (1) the time required to provide a specific repair service was difficult to predict, and (2) skilled technicians were less available in the peak summer months than at other times due to vacation schedules. Other variables include the organization's capabilities and systems for meeting service specifications, and the degree to which management believes that customer expectations can be met economically.

GAP 3: THE DIFFERENCE BETWEEN
SERVICE SPECIFICATIONS AND THE LEVEL
OF SERVICE ACTUALLY DELIVERED

Even when management *does* understand customer service expectations and *does* set appropriate specifications for the service, the delivered service may still fall short of customer expectations. We refer to Gap 3—the difference between service specifications and the actual service—as the "service performance gap." The quality level at which the service is delivered is lower than that specified by management.

A principal cause of Gap 3 is when service employees lack the willingness or the ability, or both, to perform the service the way management wants it performed. Willingness to perform may be described in terms of "discretionary effort": the difference "between the maximum amount of effort and care that an individual could bring to his or her job and the minimum amount of effort required to avoid being fired or penalized."[2] In service organizations especially, employees who begin a job by giving 100 percent discretionary effort may well be giving less within weeks or months. Service work can be discouraging—too many long lines, too many unreasonable customers, too many rules and regulations, too few pats on the back. Many service providers get "beaten up" by the service role, sacrificing discretionary effort in the process.

Moreover, many service providers may not have the needed ability to perform at expected levels. Some are hired into jobs for which they are ill-prepared, simply because they agree to work for wage rates unattractive to better-prepared candidates. Others are moved into higher-level positions before they are ready because openings are created by rapid personnel turnover. Many service workers do not receive the training they require.

All of an organization's personnel fit somewhere in the *willingness/ability to perform matrix* shown in Figure 3–2. Service employees may be both willing and able to perform the service to specifications (cell 1), willing but unable (cell 2), unwilling but able (cell 3), or unwilling and unable (cell 4). A financial institution with many employees in cells 2, 3, and 4 will have a mediocre or poor quality reputation.

Some Specific Causes of Gap 3

Among the specific factors affecting employee willingness and ability to perform the service are role conflict, dispersion of control over the service, role ambiguity, inadequate role support, and inadequate attention to middle managers.

Role Conflict

Role conflict occurs for service providers when there is a poor fit among different aspects of their jobs. One form of role conflict occurs when service providers perceive inconsistencies between demands customers make on them and demands management makes on them. The situation described in Chapter 1, of management asking tellers to be sellers and customers wanting tellers to move the line, illustrates this type of role conflict. Tellers who slow up the line to cross-sell services may be doing

FIGURE 3–2
Willingness/Ability to Perform the Service

Willingness/Ability to Perform the Service

	Unwilling to Perform Service	Willing to Perform Service
Able to Perform Service	3	1
Unable to Perform Service	4	2

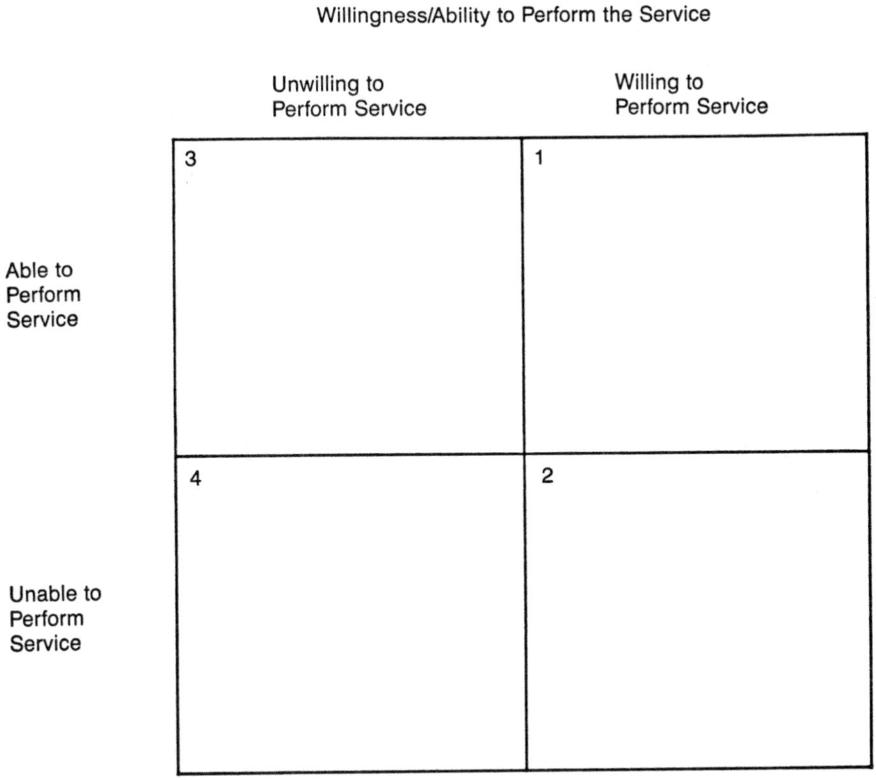

what management wants them to do, but only rarely will they be doing what customers want. Thus, tellers are thrust into the "no win" circumstance of displeasing customers to please management—a circumstance that can compromise enthusiasm and commitment for a work role.

Another type of role conflict is when there are too many competing demands placed on service providers. It is not so much that customers want one thing and managers another, as that managers assign too many roles to service providers and it is difficult for them to perform all of these roles at the level expected. The following focus group* comment from a branch banker illustrates this: "You are supposed to give your customer your undivided attention, but you have already been interrupted seven times by telephone calls. You can't put the telephone caller on hold or send him elsewhere, because once I did that and the caller was a 'shopper' and my (performance) score was lowered."

When one's work role is incompatible, the resulting sense of frustration can lead to reduced discretionary effort, absenteeism, and/or turnover—and unsatisfactory service performance from both management's and the customer's perspectives.

Dispersion of Control

Another potential cause of Gap 3 is when control over the service is dispersed among multiple parties. That is, service providers are dependent on the services of others in the organization to fully satisfy their own customers' requirements. Thus, Gap 3 problems may occur not only because contact personnel do not come through for their customers, but also because internal service providers in the organization do not come through for customer contact personnel.

When financial institutions centralize certain operations by taking them out of branch offices, they may well encounter service quality problems that offset the hoped-for productivity gains from specialization. As one banker warns in our survey for this book, "Whenever the work is moved further from the point at which the customer is served, there is greater risk that it will not be done with the customer in mind."

Consider the case of a large financial institution that stripped branch lenders of credit decision authority, shifting the authority to personnel in remote loan centers who processed completed loan applications sent by branch lenders. The loan decision and its timing were no longer in the hands of branch lenders interacting with customers. Branch personnel who had once controlled this service were now dependent

---

*The focus group quotes presented in this chapter are from a study described in Leonard L. Berry, A. Parasuraman, and Valarie Zeithaml, "The Service-Quality Puzzle," *Business Horizons*, July-August 1988.

on personnel in a distant facility. This dispersion of control over the service complicated its delivery, leading to paperwork snafus and backlogs. One branch lender said in a focus group, "My Number-1 problem is working with other units over which I have no control." A branch manager put it this way: "We're offering terrible service now. We used to have control and now we don't. We used to know where everything was and now we don't."

Another consequence of this centralization/specialization decision was that branch lenders lost esteem and clout in the eyes of their customers. The human cost of the new system was clearly expressed by one bank executive who observed, "The branch people used to be bankers but aren't anymore. All of their status, all of their recognition, is gone."[3]

The lesson from this example is not that a centralized/ specialist approach to service delivery is always the wrong thing to do. The bank in question clearly added to its woes with poor execution, probably because performance standards acceptable to both branch staff and loan center were never developed. Rather, the lesson is to keep control over the quality of service delivered as undiluted and close to the customer as possible—and be prepared for additional service quality problems when this is not the case.

Role Ambiguity

Role ambiguity occurs when employees do not have the information they need to understand their jobs adequately. Causes include employee uncertainty about what management expects, how to satisfy those expectations, and/or how their performance will be evaluated and rewarded.

Research with salespeople in various industries indicates that role ambiguity results in lower overall job satisfaction and performance.[4] Role clarity is important to service employees in nonselling roles as well. John H. Rowley, Vice President and Division Manager of Atlantic Financial in West Virginia, comments that a key obstacle to improved service quality in financial institutions is the confusion of customer contact personnel about their jobs because of multiple duties in job descriptions. He states, "I stress to our tellers that their job is to process customer financial transactions fast, accurately, and in a friendly manner. I ask them to master this basic role and not to worry about being a jack-of-all-trades."

Role ambiguity is related to, but distinct from, role conflict. In the case of role ambiguity, service providers do not fully understand their role. In the case of role conflict, service providers may know what they are supposed to do, yet view elements of the role to be in disharmony. Sometimes role conflict and ambiguity are intertwined, jeopardizing discretionary effort and performance capability all the more. Continuing with an earlier illustration, tellers who are asked to "cross-sell" in addition to processing customer transactions and who are *not* provided a clear definition of this selling role (what cross-selling means, when to do it, when not to do it) will likely experience role conflict *and* role ambiguity simultaneously.

Inadequate Role Support

Role conflict, role ambiguity, and dispersed control over the service can all contribute to Gap 3 problems. So can a lack of institutional support for a given service role, as reflected in hiring practices, training, and technology. Inadequate role support occurs when given roles in the organization are regularly staffed with people lacking the capabilities to perform them, when people in these roles do not receive the training they require, and/or when management fails to invest in appropriate technology to facilitate role performance.

Inadequate role support is a common failing in financial institutions. In the area of selection and hiring, who can argue with the notion that the quality of the worker affects the quality of work? Yet too few institutions truly invest the time and resources necessary to first define service quality standards for each job classification, and then to make sure that hiring criteria, methods, and compensation packages are sufficient to attract new hires who will meet the standards. Too many institutions are simply too lax about whom they put in front of customers!

"When we hire young people today, they often come to us without any experience or understanding of what customer service is," states an Ohio banker. "These are the 'self-service, fast-food' kids who have not had any experience with service quality as an issue. They are used to receiving shoddy service." Adds a Michigan banker, "We have required branch employees to be operationally proficient, but have not selected customer contact staff on the basis of their interpersonal skills, warm and outgoing personalities, or ability to resolve conflict."

Jim Daniel, President of Friendly Bank in Oklahoma City, refers to the *tenacity* that the selection process requires in a service business but is often missing:

> A continual challenge is finding people to hire who have the qualities necessary to provide the top-notch customer service that we require. Creative interviewing techniques must be utilized to obtain a clear picture of how the applicant truly feels about the public. Most applicants have had some degree of customer contact in previous employment. However, very few really *thrive* on customer contact. We look until we find *that* person.

Whereas selection of personnel determines the personal development potential of an institution's employees, the institution's support of training influences the personal development that actually occurs. In many institutions, training is treated in the context of "events"—a three-day training session here, a special training module there—instead of a never-ending "process" that includes ongoing management reinforcement and motivation. To assume that service personnel are "trained" when they complete a certain regimen of educational and on-the-job experiences is a trap. Service providers risk staleness, sloppiness, and lost motivation as soon as they stop growing in skills and knowledge. Training—like service quality—is a journey and not a destination.

Insufficient attention to the skills and knowledge development of service providers clearly affects their ability and willingness to perform the expected service. The following statements from branch bank employee focus groups illustrate the hazards of training that is too little and too late:

CUSTOMER-SERVICE REPRESENTATIVE:

> It's really embarrassing—customers know about new products before we do. We're the bank. We should know things be-

fore the customer does. But the training classes may be scheduled after the product comes out.

LENDING OFFICERS:

> "The bank will put out a product we don't understand—especially loans—and not tell us enough about it, not train us enough to sell it. With 'XYZ,' for example, I still have to get out the book (to look up how the loan works) and it takes me a good 10 minutes." At this point, another participant chimes in: "I just found out two weeks ago that we had the book." And then another says: "I just found out now that we had 'XYZ'!"

A third role support tool is technology. The appropriate technology can be a great "liberating" force for service providers, helping them to work smarter, faster, or more creatively. The relationship among technology, service role support, and service quality is very important. To see this, one needs only to compare a new accounts customer-service representative seated at a typewriter, completing separate forms for each service the customer buys, with a representative at another bank who opens new accounts on a CRT, inputting all data from the customer in a single computerized file at one time.

Insufficient technical support of a role can result in wasted effort, poor productivity, incomplete responses to customer service requests, and reduced time for customers because so much effort is devoted to paperwork. However, just as too little technology—or the wrong kind—will produce disappointing results, the right kind of technology may fare no better if it is improperly presented to its users or if users are not prepared properly to use it. Consider the following comment by a respondent to our survey that will close out this section on a most sobering note:

> My CEO has okayed mammoth financial support of platform automation for 1988 that he hopes will provide us with the technological differential to separate "us" from "them" via quality service. And our operations people will have it all up and running soon, to be totally installed by the end of 1988. In 500 branches. It is awesome technology. With awesome data bases. Awesome screens. But if we do not have the right people accessing that data; with the appropriate sales and service mentalities

and the attitudes and the aptitudes to help the customer; to understand what helping is in a sales sense; and to interface with every customer in a service quality sense, then we have spent a lot of money for the wrong reason. Thus, I am busting my buns to get the screens ready for marketing and service purposes and hoping we can get the human beings in the branches up to speed in service understanding.

Our CEO was convinced the new technology would make the quality difference. This is typical. He did not concern himself, even think about, the human side of the screens until I showed him the reality of the thing. As a numbers type, he assumed all these data would be used appropriately to provide that better service. No money . . . repeat . . . no money has been allocated to change the human side. Millions have gone into technology.

Overlooking Middle Managers

The leadership qualities possessed by one's manager directly influence the quality of service one delivers. One key group that is often overlooked in financial institution quality improvement efforts is middle managers—the people for whom frontline service providers work.

Discussions on quality improvement tend to center on senior management and frontline service personnel (customer contact and operations staff). Indeed, this has been the focus thus far in the chapter. Senior executives have the influence to provide the cultural emphasis that superior service quality demands. Contact and operations personnel actually perform the services customers buy. Both senior executives and frontline service providers clearly warrant the attention given them. However, it is equally true that top managers work *through* middle management, and frontline service providers work *for* middle management. Efforts to improve quality will be thwarted if these middle-level executives are left out in the cold.[5]

One of the toughest service quality challenges is *sustaining* high quality through the day and over weeks, months, and years. When the lines in the lobby are backed up to the door and there are still three more hours to go on the shift, and when the credit card customer telephones to indicate that charges on the statement belong to someone else, and it's the 23rd call of that type already received, the potential for robot-like or insensitive service—and customer disappointment—is high. The managers in the operating units in which such services are being performed are best positioned to help service providers rise to the challenge; they are best positioned to observe, coach, cajole, challenge, and inspire frontline service workers.

Too often, however, financial institution executives consider only technical skills in placing individuals into managerial slots. Leadership qualities and a service-minded attitude often are overlooked. Moreover, managers may be excluded from training and other programs directed at service improvement. Middle managers, with the best opportunity to influence the willingness and ability of service providers, are being bypassed in the service quality journey, and it is a glaring mistake. One banker makes the point in no uncertain terms in our survey:

> The weakest link in banks, which is an undermining factor of service quality, is middle management. That's where it falls apart. This comes from high turnover at this level, lack of commitment, lack of understanding "the big picture," lack of motivation, and lack of senior management communications. If service quality is ultimately provided by lower levels—tellers, proof operators, transit clerks, loan processors, and the like —then managers of these people are the enforcing link, as well as the promoting link.

GAP 4: THE DIFFERENCE BETWEEN THE DELIVERED SERVICE AND EXTERNAL COMMUNICATIONS ABOUT THE SERVICE

Gap 4 concerns a possible discrepancy between the actual service and what customers are told about the service. Many service organizations fall prey to the promotional temptations of promising better service than they can consistently deliver. Service promises made in advertising or by salespeople are broken; customers are told to expect one level of service, but actually receive another.

The temptation to overpromise in external communications is strong, since marketing personnel may be evaluated and rewarded on the basis of the new business they generate. Under these circumstances, promotional restraint and caution may not be the watchword. It is all the more difficult to clamp down on persuasive "hype" if competitors are showing no such restraint in their communications—a real possibility in deregulated times.

Using promotion to paint a rosy picture of the service may indeed lead to more initial business from customers. Unfortunately, when the institution falls short of its promises, the customer's impression of the service—and the credibility of further promotional efforts—is lowered. As Berry writes:[6]

> The "on-time" airline, the "24-hour loan" bank, the "it will be ready by five" auto repair shop, and the "no-surprises" hotel chain all encourage the customer's wrath when they fall short of these promises. It is far better to promise less and fulfill the commitment than to promise more and fall short.

Overpromising in promotion is especially pernicious because raised customer expectations affect perceptions of the service. Customers with high expectations for the service have more room for disappointment than those whose expectations are more moderate.*

CLOSING GAPS 1 TO 4

Gaps 1 to 4 constitute the major roadblocks to a successful service quality journey. Customers' service quality judgments are a function of what they desire from a service and what they perceive the service to be. Gap 5, the potential gap between the desired and perceived service, is a result of Gaps 1 to 4. Thus, by closing Gaps 1 to 4, a financial institution can close Gap 5.

We learned in Chapter 2 that key to achieving a reputation for excellent service quality is to meet or exceed customer

---

*In this paragraph we are using the term "expectations" to mean what customers "think" will happen in the service situation.

service desires. Service customers expect service organizations to look good and to be reliable, responsive, reassuring, and empathetic. The challenge then is to meet or exceed precise target market expectations for these five dimensions of service performance. Gaps 1 to 4 prevent an institution from meeting this challenge.

In this chapter, we presented the discussion of service gaps from the perspective of gap *shortfalls*, i.e., behavior in the organization is less than optimum. We took this approach to simplify and clarify the functioning of the model in Figure 3–1, and to focus on the theme of the chapter, "what gets in the way of service quality."

It is important to note, however, that Gaps 1 to 4 may occur in either direction (e.g., employees can exceed service specifications, the institution can underpromise rather than overpromise). It is possible for Gap 5 to be in either direction (i.e., customer perceptions fall short of or exceed expectations). Realistically, consistently meeting customer desires is a tough enough challenge, and financial institutions that accomplish this will be appreciated by their customers and will reap the benefits enumerated in Chapter 1.

The service quality journey involves ongoing efforts at minimizing service gaps. Successfully negotiating this journey requires genuine leadership; managership is insufficient. Service mediocrity is far easier to achieve than service superiority. Only true leaders—at the top and throughout the organization—can inspire the personal commitments needed to achieve service superiority. It is for this reason that we refer often to the issue of leadership in this book and, in Chapter 5, devote the entire chapter to it.

NOTES

1. Parasuraman, A., Valarie A. Zeithaml, and Leonard L. Berry. "A Conceptual Model of Service Quality and Its Implications for Future Research." *Journal of Marketing*, Fall 1985.
2. Yankelovich, Daniel, and John Immerwahr. *Putting the Work Ethic to Work*. New York, NY: Public Agenda Foundation, 1983.

3. Berry, Leonard L., A. Parasuraman, and Valarie A. Zeithaml. "The Service-Quality Puzzle." *Business Horizons*, July–August, 1988.
4. Berry, Leonard L., Charles M. Futrell, and Michael R. Bowers. *Bankers Who Sell*. Homewood, IL: Dow Jones-Irwin, 1985.
5. Berry, Leonard L. "Include Middle Managers in the Quest for Quality." *American Banker*, September 23, 1987, p. 4.
6. Berry, Leonard L. "Communication Central to Customer Service." *American Banker*, March 11, 1987.

CHAPTER 4

SERVICE LESSONS FROM OTHER INDUSTRIES

You ought to treat people right; its a matter of morality. The way you treat people inside manifests itself in the way you treat people outside. And if you treat them lousy inside, they're going to respond the same way in handling passengers,
—*Herbert D. Kelleher, Chairman, Southwest Airlines*[1]

Financial institutions are not alone in their drive to build customer relationships through service excellence. Many service businesses find it more cost-effective to increase volume by retaining and doing more business with existing customers than it is to attract new customers. Financial institution executives can learn much from their counterparts in other service businesses.

In this chapter, we look at four "winners" that have valuable lessons to offer the financial-services industry: Randall's Food and Drugs, Crate & Barrel, Southwest Airlines, and the Park Hyatt Hotel, Washington, D.C. In each case, the industries represented by these firms—food retailing, housewares retailing, air travel, and lodging—offer notable parallels to the financial-services industry. Each of these industries is characterized by fierce competition, labor intensity, dependence on repeat business, high overhead, and competitors who market similar goods and services. Furthermore, a good idea in one of these companies—a new service, a new way of displaying merchandise—is often quickly copied by the competition. Yet these "winning" companies continue to stay one step ahead. How do they do it? What do they have in common? What can we learn from them?

RANDALL'S: THRIVING ON CHANGE

Randall's Food and Drugs competes through constant innovation, a long-range business strategy—and service. With this combination, the Houston-based grocery chain continues to expand in a market hard hit by a substantial economic downturn.

Randall's started in 1966 with two 10,000 square foot stores. By the late 1970s, the chain was opening four or five new stores each year, largely in newly developing areas of Houston, keeping pace with the city's boom-town economy. By the mid-1980s, the oil boom was over and several major supermarket chains were forced to leave the Houston area because of poor performance. Randall's, however, continues to expand. With 39 stores at the end of 1987, Randall's had over 20 percent market share in Houston, second only to a national chain with twice as many stores. Randall's volume has increased five-fold in the past 10 years.

Staying Close to the Customer

Steering a growing organization through hard economic times requires a strong hand on the tiller and enough agility to adapt to changing market conditions. That is certainly true of Randall's. Much of the company's success is due to Chairman and co-founder Robert Onstead, who believes in hands-on leadership and open channels of communication. Instead of writing memos, Onstead makes a point of visiting the stores frequently, observing, taking notes, and talking with both customers and employees. He also personally reads and answers the numerous customer letters received each week through Randall's "We Want to Know" program.

"I can sit in my office reading computer printouts all day and not know what's going on," Onstead says. "How in the world can you get your employees to be interested in your customers if you are not interested in your employees?"[2]

Onstead leads by example, and his philosophy of staying close to the customer extends downward through the organization. District managers are assigned only five or six stores, making it possible for them to visit each one daily. "We do not believe in a large headquarters staff," says President Randall Onstead. "We like to have a lot of people out in the field, making sure store conditions are at their best."[3]

In addition, individual store managers are required to spend most of their time on the selling floor, communicating with customers and solving problems. Store manager stations in each store are highly visible and always manned, so customers know where to go if a problem arises. Store personnel take charge of servicing the shelves themselves, a duty that falls to outside suppliers in many chains, particularly for nonfood product categories. One reason is the belief that well-trained, motivated personnel can do a better job in maintaining shelves and managing inventory. The other reason is service.

"Friendly, helpful service is part of the company philosophy," explains Vice President Bill Sullins, Randall's nonfoods director. "That's not just talk. We believe in it and act on it. Our customers have come to expect that we're much more than a cold self-service store. Nonfoods plays a part in this. Having our own clerks working in the aisles enables us to assist the customer—and not just in the nonfoods aisle, but anywhere in the store."[4]

Service excellence is also the norm at checkout—where speed, accuracy, and courtesy are critical. Randall's prides itself on the friendliness of its checkers and on its commitment to minimize customer waiting time during checkout. An industry leader in the use of electronic scanners at checkout stations, Randall's policy is to immediately open unmanned stations if customers are waiting in other lines. And by issuing customer courtesy cards and installing check-verification terminals at each station, Randall's has made paying by check faster and safer for customer and store alike.

Randall's service culture works because it's practiced every day, from the top down. Robert Onstead's management style is an example that results in strong employee morale. That, in turn, translates into top-level service for the customer.

Details Make a Difference

Randall's service philosophy extends to an emphasis on detail, which, combined with the friendliness and availability of store personnel, is intended to provide a "user-friendly" environment for customers. When Robert Onstead visits a store, he looks in the corners—in the nooks and crannies—rather than in the middle of the store. "I've always been one to major in minors," he comments, "Little things make the difference; little things set us apart."[2]

Little things like:

- The brightest parking lot lights of any Houston food chain.
- The use of double-wall paper bags for sacking groceries. They cost more, but they never tear.
- Safety belts for infants in shopping carts.
- Motorized shopping carts for handicapped customers.
- Public restrooms in the sales area at all stores.
- A "Cookie Credit Card" for children, worth a free cookie at Randall's bakery.
- A dress code for employees.
- Spotless store entrances, because Robert Onstead thinks the entrances to his stores should be as clean as the entrance to his home.[2]

Little things yes, but they do add up. In an industry characterized by product and pricing sameness, these little things differentiate Randall's from its competitors. Randall's market share proves it.

Staying Ahead of the Competition

Doing the little things right is important, but so is doing the right big things! Central to the Randall's success story is management's belief—from the beginning—that the company must be longsighted in preparing a business strategy. "In the early 1980s, we vowed to be the market-share leader in Houston," Robert Onstead says. "To accomplish that, we had to open more stores."[5]

But not just any stores. "Why not win more of the customer's spending income?" Onstead asked. "When they come in for groceries, produce, and meat, why not offer film-finishing, expanded lines of general merchandise on a big scale, as well as floral and takeout foods."[6]

Instead of copying formulas that made other food stores a success, Randall's created "combo-store" operations for one-stop shopping, which today are widely imitated by competing chains in the Houston area. Randall's was one of the first supermarket chains in the country to assimilate pharmacies, delicatessens, video rental services, and appliance sales into their stores.

In addition to standard grocery items and the above-mentioned services, Randall's stores feature bakeries, floral centers, fresh seafood departments, salad bars, and cosmetic/nonfood departments—each designed for maximum eye appeal. In addition, most stores include savings and loan branches. Randall's readiness for change and innovation, like the company's attention to detail and reputation for service, is built-in. Finding new and better ways of doing business has been an ongoing management priority. Robert Onstead states, "I don't want the competitors making decisions for us."[2]

And they don't. Randall's is successful because the company's management stays in close touch with customers and employees, works hard at doing the little things right, and recognizes that strategic change is a necessary part of meeting customer expectations. As Vice President Bill Sullins says, "If we don't make fairly significant changes every quarter, I think we must be overlooking something."[7]

CRATE & BARREL: AIMING TO BE THE BEST, NOT THE BIGGEST

Would-be imitators of Crate & Barrel stores are not successful because they "miss the point," according to Gordon Segal, founder of the Chicago-based housewares chain of 25 stores. "The point is the quality of the total environment and the objective of serving the customer with a proprietary product at a unique price," Segal explains. "Too many of the people who tried to copy us went for price and did not worry about quality or went for quality and did not worry about price. And usually they did not put the right people together to make it happen. If they did, they would try to multiply it too quickly, and then they failed, because their people lacked the necessary experience. Their goals were not really to serve the customer, but to make money as fast as possible. Our goals are not driven by economics, but a need to be a superb retailer."[8]

There is not much question that Segal is a superb retailer. Retired Neiman-Marcus Chairman Stanley Marcus calls him "one of the great merchants of this century." Marcus goes on to make the distinction that Crate & Barrel is merchandise-oriented, whereas most department stores are merchandising-oriented. "Gordon makes a profit, but profit is not his first priority. He just plain loves to display his wares, and that kind of love is contagious."[9]

Serving People with Good Taste and No Money

The Crate & Barrel success story began in 1962, when Segal and his wife Carole opened the first store in an abandoned elevator factory in Chicago's Old Town neighborhood. Because they could not afford fixtures, the Segals made displays by turning over the crates and barrels in which the merchandise had been shipped.

"We were a young couple who had good taste and no money," Segal says. "We reasoned that there had to be other people with good taste and no money, so there had to be a market for a store that would service people who wanted well-designed home furnishings—especially tabletop and culinary equipment for the kitchen—but who could not afford the high-priced brands sold by fine department stores or expensive design boutiques."

Nor did the Segals have any retailing experience. "We literally didn't know a markup from a markdown," Segal admits. "We even forgot to buy a cash register on opening day. We did have some good things going for us. I was good with organizational systems and had somewhat of a business sense, and Carole, a former school teacher, was superb with design, table settings, and merchandising. We had energy, enthusiasm, and drive."[10]

Aiming for Perfection

According to Segal, the secret of Crate & Barrel's success is a business philosophy that aims for perfection in selecting and displaying merchandise, hiring and educating employees, and dealing with customers. It is the selection and display of merchandise, however, that has made Crate & Barrel one of America's most widely imitated retailing operations.

"We can sell merchandise less expensively at Crate & Barrel, because we are both an importer and a retailer," Segal says. "We import about 75 to 80 percent of the products we sell. Consequently, we don't have a wholesaler or distributor taking a markup between us and the overseas factory. That was one of our original objectives in this business. We went overseas and found small factories that we could buy from direct, doing the importing ourselves. That way, we were able to offer a much better price to our customers, a better margin for ourselves, and a better selection and variety for everyone.[11]

There are two criteria for Crate & Barrel merchandise: it must be well designed, and it must be reasonably priced. Even successful items will be dropped if they do not fit Crate & Barrel's requirement for tastefulness. "A Crate buyer ordered our ceramic handle fruit-motif spreaders without Gordon's approval," one supplier recalls. "Over 300 dozen moved within two weeks. But when Gordon saw them, he refused to reorder."[12]

Segal's meticulousness also extends to store ambience—kitchenware piled floor to ceiling, rough sawed pine, bolts of hanging cloth, soft music, theatrical lighting, theme displays, and signs that summarize a product's use, origin, and value. When he visits a store, he pays attention to the smallest details, from finger prints on the window to whether the coffee cups on display are all arranged with their handles facing in the same direction.

Customers absorb the Crate & Barrel attitude. The owner of a competing firm recalled watching a customer at a wood display in a Crate & Barrel store. "He picked up a tray, then put it down and walked away. He must have realized he did something wrong because suddenly he turned around, went back to the display, and adjusted the tray. Obviously, Gordon's attention to detail is infectious. In my store, the customer looks at a tray, then throws it on the floor."[12]

Building Relationships

Merchandise—carefully selected, reasonably priced, and beautifully displayed—is one cornerstone of Crate & Barrel's success story. The other, Segal believes, is the company's ability to build and maintain relationships with both customers and employees.

Crate & Barrel's first commitment is to serve as a buying agent for the customer. "Our customers think of Crate & Barrel as a place where you can always find something—where you can get great value and find beautiful things in a friendly atmosphere."[13]

Selling in the stores is practiced as an "educational process." Sales people are expected to know the product and educate the consumer about it, which Segal believes has more impact in creating a relationship than either advertising or displays. "We want our customers for the long-term; we don't want them just for the sale of today," he explains. "If they can't take one of our products home and use it and enjoy it, we prefer they bring it back and either exchange it for something else or return it for a refund."[13]

Creating an environment—and an attitude—that keeps customers coming back begins with employees who are enthusiastic about and interested in what they do. Each store functions as its own little company, and each store manager is responsible for hiring and training staff. Crate & Barrel does not hire people who have worked for other retail companies —and who may have acquired bad habits. Moreover, every newly hired employee starts the way Gordon and Carole Segal started—doing everything.

"Decentralized management requires, above all, the ability to attract the right people," Segal states. "Most everyone who works in our stores or our corporate headquarters has attended college. Each associate is hired to be a merchant and a future leader, not just a sales clerk. We put our best people on the front line, and that's where we're different. We interview 10 or 12 people for every 1 we hire. We spend a lot of time choosing a certain type of person with a certain talent, taste, and style. The most important ingredient to Crate & Barrel is absolutely these associates and the beliefs we engender in them."[14]

As a result of this effort, Crate & Barrel boasts a remarkable employee retention record. Most people in key positions have been with Crate & Barrel for 10 to 15 years, and in the entire history of the organization, only one store manager has ever been lost to the competition.

Keeping the Customer Focus

Hiring bright young people is one thing. Keeping them motivated day-to-day and helping them to grow is another. Training—both formal and informal—receives primary emphasis at Crate & Barrel. Responsibility for training is divided between in-store efforts and a company-wide continuing education program.

The corporate training program involves three phases. For "Fundamentals of Selling," the first phase, employees travel to company headquarters in groups of 10 or so for sessions on corporate structure and philosophy, how to relate to customers, salesmanship, add-on sales, how buyers find new products, and other topics. Phase two focuses on product information, with sessions broken into different product categories, such as gourmet cookware, dinnerware, and glassware. Phase three covers store design—merchandising philosophy, traffic flow, the effects of high and low crates, window display, and so on.

The constant in all training is the philosophy of customer focus—the philosophy of excellence in product, store, service, and value. As Segal stated in a 1987 speech, "The great retail companies have a philosophy, a mission, and they take the time to share this with the staff. . . . It amazes me that retailers talk so much about service, but spend so little time bringing up and training their people."[15]

Gordon and Carole Segal started with a good idea for which there was an underserved market niche. They added a sense of style and design—and attention to detail—that set an industry standard. They established excellent customer service as a primary goal, and then built and trained a sales organization that could deliver the level of service they demanded. Their overriding ambition was to be the best, not the biggest, to please customers—and themselves—not follow the competition, teach and bring along employees, and create a "family" culture, not just sell jobs to young people. In 1988, as this book goes to press, the Segals are still at it, still enjoying it, still practicing retailing "their way."

SOUTHWEST AIRLINES: THE FAMILY THAT FLIES TOGETHER

Every chief executive likes to hear the service excellence of his company extolled. However, Herbert D. Kelleher, Chairman of Southwest Airlines, must have had mixed feelings the day he received a phone call from his sister-in-law regarding the superb service she had received on a Southwest flight. When Kelleher asked how many passengers had been on the flight, his sister-in-law answered that there were two pilots, three flight attendants—and herself.[16]

That was in 1971, when the newly formed airline was struggling to stay alive on its three-city Texas route against competition from three other carriers. By 1987, Southwest was serving 26 cities in 12 states with more than 650 flights each day. Assets had exceeded $1 billion, and earnings over the previous five years had surpassed $206 million. In spite of this rapid growth, Southwest's reputation for service excellence remains undiminished; its complaints-per-passengers-flown ratio is regularly the lowest in the industry.

Here, again, the success story of an organization rests on the strength and vision of its leadership and its ability to thrive in a highly competitive environment. Southwest Airlines was born in 1967, the brainchild of San Antonio entrepreneur Rollin W. King and his attorney Herbert D. Kelleher. The cocktail napkin on which the proposed triangular Houston-Dallas-San Antonio commuter route was first sketched hangs today on a plaque in Kelleher's office, along with the words, "Herb, let's start an airline," and "Rollin, you're crazy. Let's do it!"[17]

That was the easy part. Over the next several years, Kelleher was forced to defend Southwest's right to exist—and do business its own way—in court battles that reached all the way to the U.S. Supreme Court. The first challenge came from competing airlines, who claimed that the three cities Southwest wanted to serve could not support a new carrier. The next fight was over Southwest's right to fly from the centrally located Love Field in Dallas—as opposed to the newer but less convenient Dallas-Fort Worth Regional Airport.

Through it all, Southwest met the competitive challenge head on with marketing innovations designed to attract customers, such as different fares for day and evening flights and a guaranteed 10-minute turnaround between flight arrival and departure. It wasn't long, however, before competing carriers copied Southwest's fare structures. In addition, following Southwest's lead to remain at Houston's downtown Hobby Airport, competing airlines moved part of their service back to Hobby to fight Southwest on its own ground. But by the mid-1970s, they were gone.

The reason, according to Kelleher, was "better service —prompter, faster, with no late planes and no slow lines at the ticket counter and a 10-minute turnaround. And then, of course, we would write things and put them on the planes . . . just things reminding them that Braniff and Texas International would never have reduced their fares if we hadn't come into Hobby with our low fares first. We suggested they fly us whenever they could, because we were the only thing they had to keep the other guy honest."[18]

Competition Helped Forge the Southwest Family

Herb Kelleher thrives on competition, believing that in a free market, the problems of one organization can become opportunities for competitors able to provide new or better service. He also believes that Southwest's early troubles helped forge its employees into a close-knit family. "It made us very close, the original employees and those who came along shortly thereafter," he says. "It made us very competitive. It made us quick-response minded because if we didn't respond quickly, we were done. It made us, I think, innovative. We had to innovate out of necessity. And it made us very cost conscious, which, I think, is the primary prerequisite for being successful from a financial standpoint. And that has persisted as more or less a tradition within the company."[19]

That closeness remains today as perhaps the most important aspect of Southwest Airline's internal culture, a culture in which no one gets preferential treatment. Vice President Colleen Barrett, who came to Southwest 20 years ago after having worked as a legal secretary for Herb Kelleher, recalls an incident that she still relates to people who report to her: "I had worked for law firms all my life, and it was not at all unusual for me to be in the office at 10:00 P.M. stuffing envelopes. The first time I did such a mailing for Herb, he was sitting on the floor at 2:00 A.M. stuffing envelopes too! That's the way he is. He would never ask somebody to work harder than he does. He's not above stapling or copying documents—doing whatever the job takes. He's a real team player, and I think that *is* leadership by example."

The sense of "family" is encouraged by a management structure that is short on bureaucracy and long on personal interaction. "Herb hates bureaucracy," Barrett says. "He lets people run their own departments, and he respects their jurisdiction. About the only time he interferes is when he thinks something is becoming too bureaucratic or dictatorial, or when the employees are not being treated properly. Nobody has assistants, and there are very few committees at Southwest. Most of those are short-lived project committees. When the problem is solved, the committee is dissolved."

This lean organizational structure, which enables the airline to react quickly to market shifts and customer needs, is an approach to management that Kelleher believes will characterize those airlines able to survive in a highly competitive environment. "I think we must create the feeling that it's 'one for all and all for one,' a sort of 'Three Musketeers' family feeling where there's a willingness to sacrifice and take care of each other in order to prosper. That way we'll bring on new generations of employees who will have very secure, well paying, enjoyable, and fun jobs," he says.[20]

Kelleher, who is "Herb" to Southwest's approximately 6,000 employees, is not just talking when he speaks of a "Three Musketeers feeling." He leads by example. His willingness to pitch in—to work in the rain all night with baggage handlers on a busy Wednesday before Thanksgiving, for example—is part of company lore. He's approachable. He knows what is going on. He communicates. He is a true service champion.

"You have to have your heroes," Barrett comments. "And people know when it's not real. We once had an officer at Southwest who said all the right things—in every letter, every time he made a speech to employees. But he wasn't sincere. It took the employees about three months to see that. You can't put it on paper, then walk down the hall with your nose to the floor, not saying hello to people, and still say you're a family person. It just doesn't work that way."

Communication: The Personal Touch

Herb Kelleher earns the respect of his people by practicing what he preaches. He finds out what his employees need by roaming the company to talk with them, making sure he includes each department. He shows his appreciation by taking over restaurants for company celebrations. He remembers employee birthdays with cards, and employee illnesses with cards or flowers. He remembers employees' names. He makes sure that key decisions are discussed with employees first.

More formal rituals and channels of communication also work at Southwest. *Luv Lines*, the monthly employee publication, reflects the "Love" trademark that has been part of the company's advertising and other promotions since it won its court battle to remain at Dallas' Love Field in the early 1970s. Issues of *Luv Lines* focus on Southwest's employees, reminding them of company values and spotlighting those who best exemplify those values. One column is devoted to "Winning Spirit

Award" recipients, employees who are honored each month for extraordinary service with pins, certificates, and Southwest passes.

The list goes on. An annual banquet and awards ceremony. Special events, such as a lavish "Spirit of Kitty Hawk" party celebrating the purchase of more fuel-efficient aircraft. A "Help Herb" campaign that works because employees know that suggestions they send in will be read and acted upon.

One result is that Southwest is a company for which it is "fun" to work. Robert Lawless, Chief Operating Officer, elaborates: "Southwest from the beginning wanted to focus on 'fun.' That was going to be the difference, and that is still the focus today. Every candidate for employment is screened by a personality profile—for fun, teamwork, and a people-oriented attitude. Even pilots who are technically qualified are not hired if they don't fit the personality profile." Lawless adds, "Fares are the same, planes are the same—only the people are different."[21]

The Customer as "Family"

One of Herb Kelleher's favorite stories is about Gigi Perry, a Southwest ticket agent in Dallas. Leaving the airport one night, Perry encountered a stranded passenger on the curb, a 70-year-old woman bound for Amarillo, who had been grounded in Dallas because of fog. The woman had missed the bus taking stranded passengers to a hotel and had been waiting on the curb for hours. Perry drove the woman to the hotel, spent the night with her because she was afraid to be alone, then drove her back to the airport in the morning in time to catch her flight. According to Kelleher, "Our people do that type of thing all the time. I mean they have big, big hearts."[22]

To stewardess Tona Weigelt, the Southwest spirit translates into love. "We love our passengers, and we care about them . . . like you treat family, with that loving spirit." "Herb Kelleher," she went on to say, "really feels that without good employees, he's not going to have any passengers on the airplanes, and it's one of those circles where if he takes good care of the company, takes good care of his employees, his employees, in turn, take good care of the passengers."[23]

At Southwest Airlines, customer service is a natural outgrowth of a corporate culture that stresses respect for the individual. It starts at the top, with a leader who sets an example, who cares about employees and customers, and who lets them know it. And it has made Southwest Airlines a winner in a shifting, deregulated industry beset by fierce competition, bankruptcies, acquisitions, and mergers.

"Excellent customer service is surely how you win this game of inches," Kelleher said in a speech to his employees. "Where everybody else is flying airplanes, everybody else has the hardware, the software of success in the American airline industry is you. The software of success is treating our customers well, whether they be customers inside the company—and to a certain extent, you know, our departments are all customers of other departments—or whether they be customers outside the company."[24]

PARK HYATT HOTEL: EMPLOYEES MAKE THE DIFFERENCE

Discussing service quality can be a comparative exercise. Charles Shoemaker, Vice President of First National Bank of Chicago, recalls arriving in Washington, D.C., at 11:00 P.M. one Sunday only to find that his luggage had failed to make the trip with him. When he reported his problem to a representative of the airline, the response was, "I imagine they forgot to put it on the plane." Shoemaker agreed that it looked that way, and asked if it might have gone on some other plane. "I doubt it," the woman behind the counter answered. Shoemaker then asked if she could check with Chicago. "Well, I don't think anybody's there," she said. Shoemaker then said, "Look, just make me feel better. Call so we can know if the baggage is there." She called, and after about a ring and a half, said that no one was there. Then she said, "You know, we've got a flight at 10:00 tomorrow morning, and I'm sure it will be on that. Fill out this paperwork and give us a call in the morning."

It was one of those nights. When Shoemaker later arrived at Washington's Park Hyatt Hotel, he found that there was no record of his reservation. "Before I had time to produce the confirmation slip, the woman at the desk had called out the Assistant Manager, who apologized for the mistake and gave me a very nice room in compensation. I then commented that my baggage had been lost. Within minutes, the hotel produced a toothbrush and shaving kit, and the porter arrived with the newspaper. By then, I was feeling awfully good about the hotel—and the airline looked so bad."

What made the difference was people and the way they performed. For Paul Limbert, Park Hyatt's General Manager, finding the people who *would* make the difference was top priority. "When I first came here, this hotel was just a hole in the ground," he says. "We knew that the owners were going to provide us with a great box—with a hotel that was superior in construction and materials. But this hotel is just one of several in the city with marble, chandeliers, and beautiful carpets. The only thing that makes a difference is the staff."

Limbert adds that every hotel general manager in the city says the same thing—that their employees are their most important asset—but he doesn't believe them. "If that were so, why don't they talk to them?" he asks. Limbert talks to his employees, even interviewing prospective new employees at the hotel, everyone from department heads to dishwashers. For the hotel's opening in 1986, Limbert interviewed 358 new hires, culled down from more than 4,000 applicants. Before he sees them, job applicants have already been screened for their qualifications and ability to do the job. He's looking for something else.

Never Say "No"

"In hiring staff for the hotel, I have a philosophy that goes back to the days when I was a waiter," Limbert explains. "I was never a very good waiter, but I never had any complaints. Yet there were waiters far better than I who were constantly receiving complaints. In some restaurants, customers wonder if they are good enough to be there. The maitre d' looks them over to see if they are wearing the right shirt and shoes, then seats them at a table in the back of the room. The wine steward arrives to let them know how much they don't know about wine. Then the waiter lets them know they are in the wrong restaurant by making them wait for service.

"I thought, 'It's the friendly people like myself who get away with murder.' So, if you're going to staff a hotel, you should staff it with friendly people, because none of us is perfect. Many things can go wrong in a hotel—lost reservations, rooms not made up on time. We have close to 400 employees here. That's 400 people thinking and doing things their own way. So I look for friendliness, for a desire to serve, and that comes from the heart. You can teach somebody to put a plate down on the righthand side or how to pick up a water glass, but you can't teach them to be friendly."

In the final prehire interview with new employees, Limbert's first objective is to put them at ease by having them talk about their families, their lives, or whatever they want to talk about. "Then we talk about my philosophy of business, and the fact that I believe guests are always right—even if we know they're wrong," Limbert says. "After all, if you argue with someone and prove to them that they're wrong, you win the battle but lose the war, because they'll never come back. People have to know that the philosophy of 'we never say no' comes from me."

Not saying "no" is sometimes difficult. Limbert recalls a recent instance in which a party checking into the Presidential Suite required a larger dining table. When the new table was installed, however, it turned out the chandelier was hanging slightly off center. The solution was removing the chandelier and drilling new holes in the ceiling to rehang it—only hours before the guests were scheduled to arrive.

On a day-to-day basis, saying "yes" translates directly into service, attention to detail—and to repeat business. Limbert recalls one guest who always leaves his underwear and socks behind, to be laundered for his return visit. Another likes the light bulbs in his room to be replaced with bulbs of a lower wattage. Yet a third brings his own food with him, and prefers to keep it in his room in a separate refrigerator from the one already there. "I recently had a guest tell me he'd never been to a restaurant like the one in the hotel," Limbert adds. It seems one of the desserts on the menu that night was raspberry napoleon. The guest liked napoleons, but not raspberries. The waiter excused himself, went to the kitchen, and returned with the news that if the guest didn't mind waiting 20 minutes, the chef would be delighted to bake a "customized" napoleon with no raspberries.

"I think that's what it's all about," Limbert says. "I tell employees, 'If you're worried about it, do it the right way.' Sometimes it's the hard way. Sometimes it's the most expensive way. But I will never chastise anybody for doing something right—only for taking a shortcut, for doing something I consider to be substandard."

Communication: Top Down, Bottom Up

The final interview may be the first time Park Hyatt employees see the General Manager, but it isn't the last. Limbert admits that he is difficult to reach in his office because he is always walking around the hotel talking with employees, or at the front desk greeting guests. He can even be found pitching in around the hotel—helping to park cars, for example—if there are things he can do to help keep customer service at an "excellent" level.

"The Hyatt management style is characterized as 'top down, bottom up.' We listen to the staff. They are the ones who give us the customer feedback that enables us to improve," Limbert says.

Although Park Hyatt publishes a monthly employee newsletter, the most important means of communicating company values is meetings, starting with the daily "Touch Down" and weekly staff meetings. "Things change so quickly in this business that we have to be in constant communication," Limbert explains. "Brief 'Touch Down' meetings are held at the beginning of each shift to discuss impending arrivals and departures, and what incoming guests might require. They provide continuity from shift to shift. Each day, we produce 'Red Flag' reports on anything that might have inconvenienced a guest during the day. Even things mentioned in passing at the check-out desk are entered on guest reaction forms that I review for discussion at the weekly meetings."

Each month, Limbert chairs "Hyatt Talks"—forums designed to encourage upward communication between line personnel and top management. "My employees are very honest when we get middle management out of the way," he comments. "Hyatt Talks give me an opportunity to hear how the employees think we are doing. We discuss everything from treatment of employees to equipment shortages that I might not know about. And of course, we talk about what the guests think of us and how we might provide better service."

Employee training at the Park Hyatt combines self-instructional and on-the-job methods. The first step is an orientation session in which employees are introduced both to the company's service philosophy and to the operation of the hotel as a whole. Next, they are given manuals that explain the operation of their department and that take them through their specific jobs, followed by intensive "hands-on" training. Managers from various departments also conduct cross-training sessions, explaining through movies and lectures how their particular areas operate. Perhaps most important to service quality, however, is the course on communication skills taught by Limbert and other senior managers. "If you have a hotel without communication," Limbert comments, "you don't have anything."

Making Work Fun

Like Randall's, Crate & Barrel, and Southwest Airlines, the Park Hyatt Hotel is, Limbert believes, a "fun place to work." From Friday parties for employees—complete with live bands and lavish buffets—to monthly and annual awards programs that honor outstanding service providers with cash prizes and vacation trips, the hotel's management strives to create a work environment from which excellent service is a natural outgrowth.

"We believe in paying people well and in rewarding outstanding performance, but we do not believe that the extra few dollars an hour makes for better service," Limbert explains. "What makes the difference is treating employees with dignity and respect. Yes, it's important that people receive their salary increases on time, but cash doesn't necessarily make for happy employees. We're all working together trying to provide the best product in town. We can do it because we let our employees know that they make the difference, and treat them accordingly."

CLOSING THE GAPS

Closing the service gaps discussed in Chapter 3 is a function of informed, service-minded leadership. Robert Onstead, Gordon Segal, Herbert Kelleher, and Paul Limbert give us a composite profile of the special qualities of true service leaders.

- They stay close to the customer, spending large amounts of time in service facilities, talking to customers directly, and seeing for themselves what goes on. They read complaint letters, answer customer phone calls, and sponsor marketing research to keep track both of what is actually happening in the organization, and market shifts that might affect its future.
- They realize, and act upon, the critical importance of upward communication. They know that line personnel are closest to the customer and have the best view of actual service levels. To tap this pool of vital information, they have implemented formal and informal methods of learning about—and addressing—service problems perceived by employees. From "management by walking around" to suggestion box programs and regular meetings with line personnel, Onstead, Segal, Kelleher, and Limbert listen to the "sounds" of their businesses.
- They personally spread the service philosophy within the organization, and serve as a role model in the process —from Paul Limbert parking cars to Herb Kelleher unloading baggage. Each champions high service standards and goals, and promotes them at every opportunity

in daily contact with employees and through formal methods of downward communication, from newsletters to meetings and special events.

- The service leader understands that the employee is the key component to providing high quality service. Each is involved in employee selection—sometimes directly— and in the orienting of new employees with the service gospel. A service leader rewards excellence, and frequently bases outstanding service awards on employees' ingenuity and their ability to solve service-related problems.

- Most important of all, service leaders have created internal cultures from which service excellence springs as a natural outgrowth. Leaders promote a sense of teamwork. They believe that the workplace should be "fun." They also believe that if employees are treated with dignity and respect, these attributes will shine through in their encounters with customers. And they are right. The service cultures are so thick at Randall's, Crate & Barrel, Southwest Airlines, and the Park Hyatt, Washington, D.C., you can cut them with a knife!

Back to the Basics

There is nothing new to this formula for success. High-performing service organizations are successful because their managements understand and stick to the basics. They are oriented toward change, quality, value, and people. Management knows the business, and runs it with an eye to the future. They are obsessed with small things as well as big things—with execution as well as strategy. Above all, they understand that serving the customer is their reason for being.

Many financial institutions are still trapped in the massive inertia of corporate cultures that are too short-term–oriented and that place too much emphasis on operational issues and cost-control at the expense of serving customers. The managements of these institutions can learn valuable lessons by taking a close look at the values and philosophies that make other service organizations great.

NOTES

1. Freiberg, Kevin L. *The Heart and Spirit of Transformational Leadership: A Qualitative Case Study of Herb Kelleher's Passion for Southwest Airlines.* Doctoral dissertation, University of San Diego, 1987, p. 283.
2. Berry, Leonard L., and George A. Rieder. "A Grocery List for Bankers—Lessons from Randall's Stores." *American Banker,* December 24, 1985, p. 4.
3. Tanner, Ronald. "Randall's: On the Expansion Trail." *Progressive Grocer,* May 1987, p. 208.
4. Snyder, Glenn. "Randall's Combos: Changing with the Times." *Progressive Grocer,* February 1987, p. 100.
5. Tanner, Ronald. "Randall's: On the Expansion Trail." *Progressive Grocer,* May 1987, p. 206.
6. Snyder, Glenn. "Randall's Combos: Changing with the Times." *Progressive Grocer,* February 1987, p. 95.
7. Snyder, Glenn. "Randall's Combos: Changing with the Times." *Progressive Grocer,* February 1987, p. 93.
8. Segal, Gordon. "Crate & Barrel: Success Develops from a Unique Idea." *International Trends in Retailing,* Fall 1986, p. 27.
9. Kahn, Joseph P. "On Display." *Inc.,* November 1985, p. 112.
10. Segal, Gordon. "Crate & Barrel: Success Develops from a Unique Idea." *International Trends in Retailing,* Fall 1986, pp. 25–26.
11. Segal, Gordon. "Crate & Barrel: Success Develops from a Unique Idea." *International Trends in Retailing,* Fall 1986, p. 28.
12. Brin, Geri, and Debra Kent. "What Makes the Crate & Barrel Work?" *Entree,* October 1984, p. 36.
13. Segal, Gordon. "Crate & Barrel: Success Develops from a Unique Idea." *International Trends in Retailing,* Fall 1986, p. 29.
14. Segal, Gordon. "Crate & Barrel: Success Develops from a Unique Idea." *International Trends in Retailing,* Fall 1986, p. 30.
15. Segal, Gordon. Presentation at the Center for Retailing Studies Symposium, Dallas, Texas, September 30, 1987.
16. Freiberg, Kevin L. *The Heart and Spirit of Transformational Leadership: A Qualitative Case Study of Herb Kelleher's Passion for Southwest Airlines.* Doctoral dissertation, University of San Diego, 1987, p. 133.
17. Freiberg, Kevin L. *The Heart and Spirit of Transformational Leadership: A Qualitative Case Study of Herb Kelleher's Passion for Southwest Airlines.* Doctoral dissertation, University of San Diego, 1987, p. 127.
18. Freiberg, Kevin L. *The Heart and Spirit of Transformational*

Leadership: A Qualitative Case Study of Herb Kelleher's Passion for Southwest Airlines. Doctoral dissertation, University of San Diego, 1987, pp. 134–135.

19. Freiberg, Kevin L. *The Heart and Spirit of Transformational Leadership: A Qualitative Case Study of Herb Kelleher's Passion for Southwest Airlines.* Doctoral dissertation, University of San Diego, 1987, p. 153.

20. Freiberg, Kevin L. *The Heart and Spirit of Transformational Leadership: A Qualitative Case Study of Herb Kelleher's Passion for Southwest Airlines.* Doctoral dissertation, University of San Diego, 1987, p. 164.

21. Lawless, Robert. Presentation at the Center for Retailing Studies Symposium, Dallas, Texas, September 30, 1987.

22. Freiberg, Kevin L. *The Heart and Spirit of Transformational Leadership: A Qualitative Case Study of Herb Kelleher's Passion for Southwest Airlines.* Doctoral dissertation, University of San Diego, 1987, pp. 237–238.

23. Freiberg, Kevin L. *The Heart and Spirit of Transformational Leadership: A Qualitative Case Study of Herb Kelleher's Passion for Southwest Airlines.* Doctoral dissertation, University of San Diego, 1987, p. 199.

24. Freiberg, Kevin L. *The Heart and Spirit of Transformational Leadership: A Qualitative Case Study of Herb Kelleher's Passion for Southwest Airlines.* Doctoral dissertation, University of San Diego, 1987, p. 238.

CHAPTER 5

SERVICE LEADERSHIP—
THE DRIVING FORCE

Show me a bank that has an ongoing program of high quality service, inside out, top to bottom, and I'll show you a unique CEO who understands human relations.
—Senior Vice President for a major regional bank

Quality service is a journey, and leadership is the driving force behind it. Leaders not only set the direction, but also provide the power that gets things started and keeps them rolling. Cultural change won't happen by itself, and without strong leadership, it is unlikely to happen at all. As consultant Gail Hoffman writes, "Quality service begins with senior management. If they are not openly committed, it is difficult, if not impossible, for their underlings to be committed. Commitment must be seen in terms of leadership, not management."[1]

Leadership is particularly important in overcoming the first great barrier to an organization-wide commitment to customer service. We call this barrier the "Service Wall," and define it as nothing less than the organization's existing culture—the shared set of values and attitudes that have developed over time, and which characterize and sometimes limit the organization and its business strategies. If an emphasis on service quality is not part of the existing culture, breaking down the Service Wall can be a formidable undertaking indeed—one that clearly has to start at the top of the organization.

As one bank executive we surveyed comments, "Leadership is really the key solution to most of the problems in banking. If you have weak management, you will have trouble selling, trouble servicing, trouble maintaining staff, and trouble with morale. The same is true of any business."

ONLY LEADERSHIP PROVIDES THE OPPORTUNITY FOR CULTURAL CHANGE

Starting the journey to improved service quality is more difficult than meets the eye. A senior management directive to "turn right" won't necessarily stop the organization from lumbering along its well established rut. "It is not that strategic initiatives are ignored, as much as it is they just do not make sense to people when viewed from the old cultural perspectives. Consequently, whenever there is a discrepancy between culture and change, culture always wins."[2]

This situation is especially problematic in financial institutions, where decades of operating in a rigidly regulated environment have created a cultural inertia that sometimes seems paralyzing. In *Thriving on Chaos,* Tom Peters writes that for American business and industry in general, the rate of change has accelerated to such an extent that the only solution is a "management revolution"—an entirely new approach to doing business in the global marketplace. One strategy, he suggests, is ". . . meeting uncertainty by emphasizing a set of new basics: world-class quality and service, enhanced responsiveness through greatly increased flexibility, and continuous, short-cycle innovation and improvement aimed at creating new markets for both new and apparently mature products and services."[3]

Although he is addressing business and industry in general with that prescription, Peters might as well be addressing the financial services industry specifically, for nowhere is the pace of change more dizzying. Nowhere is competition more fierce, quality and service more important as a means of differentiation, the "newness" of products and services more brief, or the development and maintenance of markets more critical. Responding to market and competitive turbulence with a "management revolution" may represent the financial services industry's biggest challenge.

CHARACTERISTICS OF SERVICE LEADERSHIP

Changing a corporate culture requires leaders, not managers. There *is* a difference. In their book *Leaders: The Strategies for Taking Charge,* Bennis and Nanus point out that leaders focus on the emotional and spiritual resources of the organization —on its values, commitment, and aspirations. Leaders start with a vision, and focus their efforts on turning that vision into reality. Leaders pull people, not push them.[4]

Managers, on the other hand, emphasize the physical resources of the organization—its capital resources, raw materials, and technology. Managers are more effective at administering what exists than they are at changing the status quo.

While it is possible for the same individual to be both a good leader and a good manager, the linkage between the two is no sure thing. In this book on service quality, we stress leadership—at all levels of the organization, not just the top —because only true leadership can establish service-mindedness as a cultural imperative.

True leaders:

1. Have a vision of the business.
2. Communicate their vision of the business.
3. Are entrepreneurial.
4. Are obsessed with excellence.

Leaders have other characteristics as well, but we believe these four are especially important in shaping a service-minded culture.

Leaders Have a Vision of the Business

What we mean by "vision" is a mental picture of tomorrow's organization—of what it will be, of its essential success factors, of its "reason for being." It is the vision that potentially inspires monumental achievement, that grabs hold of individual employees and makes their jobs a "calling," that "pulls" them to excellence. Leaders have the ability to see their organizations not just as they are, but as they can be—and sometimes as they must be to survive.

It was a leader's persistent vision that transformed the impossibly complex notion of building a legion of people, an airforce of planes, a fleet of vans, and an operations facility in Memphis into the reality of Federal Express and the reliable delivery of urgent mail the very next day throughout America! Only Fred Smith's inspired leadership could have turned the incredible dream of Federal Express into a reality—and, in the process, energized an entire industry for express mail.

A persistent, determined commitment to a vision characterizes leaders. That's how Lee Iaccoca turned Chrysler around. It is the power that helps keep Southwest Airlines flying high, and that has helped make Randall's and Crate & Barrel marks to be measured against in retailing.

Leaders Communicate Their Vision of the Business

Having a vision is not enough, as even the best idea is nullified if kept a secret from the people who can empower it. The vision must be constantly communicated and reinforced to give it life. True leaders devote considerable time and energy doing just that.

"The winning performers understand that actions speak louder than words—*but* they also understand that the words may have to be repeated endlessly . . . so they never stop communicating," write Clifford and Cavanaugh in their book, *The Winning Performance: How America's High-Growth Midsize Companies Succeed.* "The leaders spend prodigious hours writing, speaking, visiting the troops in outposts, doing whatever's necessary to get the essential messages across."[5]

Leadership is visible. By practicing what they preach, leaders set an example for others in the organization to follow. Gordon Segal at Crate & Barrel, Robert Onstead at Randall's, Herbert Kelleher at Southwest Airlines, and Paul Limbert at the Park Hyatt all lead in the field rather than from their desks. Service in these organizations is a byword, in part because their leaders seldom miss an opportunity to reinforce its importance in employee contact situations, from mass meetings to one-on-one encounters.

Stories about Nordstrom, the Seattle-based department store chain famous for its service, are told frequently. One of our favorites, in the book *A Passion for Excellence*,[6] is that of a Nordstrom brother who wanders into the back room of the men's shoe department on one of his frequent store visits. While there, he notices numerous gaps along the shelves in violation of the company's policy that merchandise always be in stock. The salesperson assures Mr. Nordstrom that out-of-stock items have been reordered, and holds up order forms as proof. Then, as the story goes, Mr. Nordstrom places an order form in each empty space along the shelves and states, "Why don't you wrap these forms around the customers' feet if they ask for out-of-stock items?" We tell this story here because it illustrates how leaders communicate their visions—personally, directly, believably, one-on-one, and often.

At Nordstrom, Federal Express, Southwest Airlines, and many other high-performing service organizations, excellent customer service was part of the original "vision." In each case, the organizations' founders realized that service was a critical component of growth and success. Sharing that philosophy became a personal priority. For financial institutions attempting to make the shift to service-oriented cultures, the example of leadership and how leaders communicate what is often a new priority is critical.

"The personal touch is a very powerful tool," says Lawrence Avril, CEO of Hinsdale Federal Savings and Loan. "Personal witness to service quality goes a long way toward general organizational implementation. Since we believe that significant changes in corporate culture begin most effectively at the top, we continue to influence the association environment from the top down. In short, I try to exemplify good service quality by living it."

Employees at all levels watch senior management very closely for clues as to what is important in the organization. Actions speak louder than words, but the words are important as well. Leaders underline their commitment to the vision at every opportunity, through every means of communication at their disposal, and—more importantly—through the example they set by their daily activities.

Leaders Are Entrepreneurial

True leaders look toward the future, with an eye to shaping it to their own ends. They understand that change is inevitable in pursuit of the vision, and that complacency is a killer. True leaders know that winning means changing, and they seek out change rather than just letting it happen. They reject the idea that "if it ain't broke, don't fix it." Instead, they subscribe to the notion, "If it ain't been fixed, it will break."[7]

Stew Leonard's unique food store is one of the best examples we know of fixing things before they break. The Leonard family, which founded Stew Leonard's and runs it today, serves customers with an entrepreneurial flair unmatched elsewhere in retailing. A jazz band serenades customers at the front entrance. A petting zoo is in front of the store. Employees dressed as barnyard animals and cartoon characters roam the store aisles. Restrooms are decorated with fresh flowers.

An in-store suggestion box generates more than 100 suggestions each day, to which management pays zealous attention. Top management conducts monthly focus group sessions with customers, and distributes one-page summaries of issues and action steps to all other managers the very next day!

Stew Leonard's takes care of its customers, and the customers respond. In spite of the fact that Stew Leonard's has umpteen competitors surrounding its store in Norwalk, Connecticut, the store boasts sales of $2,800 per square foot—a remarkable figure in retailing. In this store, Stew Leonard's will sell in a year's time 100 tons of cottage cheese, 1 million ice cream cones, and more than 1,000 tons of hamburger meat.

In telling the Stew Leonard's story, we are not advocating that financial institutions have their employees dress up in clown costumes or that they make spotless restrooms the Number-1 service priority. What we are advocating is leadership that continually hunts for more and better ways to serve customers, leadership that transforms what exists into something better. The magic of the Leonard family is that they have created an organizational culture of listening to customers and continually changing the firm's operations based on what is heard. The Leonard's are not only innovative in their own right, they are also innovative in encouraging others in the company to be innovative. There is no such thing as "business as usual" at Stew Leonard's.

Leaders Are Obsessed with Excellence

Leaders are driven to be "the best." We know of no term more appropriate than "obsession" to describe this characteristic of leadership. True leaders have a sense of urgency about running a first-rate operation that is palpably evident to other employees. Leaders are like top athletes; the competitive fires burn hot. Losing a customer through poor service is like losing the 100-yard dash to a bitter rival. Obsession with excellent execution is a hallmark of great leaders regardless of the organizational level at which they lead.

One example of the obsession characteristic is Dunkin' Donuts, whose drive to serve great coffee is described by Clifford and Cavanaugh in *The Winning Performance*:[8]

> Dunkin' Donuts really cares about the quality of its coffee. Its goal is to serve "the best cup of coffee in the world." Dunkin' Donuts has a 23-page specification of what it requires in a coffee bean. But buying high-quality, specially blended coffee beans is just the beginning. Dunkin' Donuts franchisees have to make sure their coffee is fresh. Beans are to be used within 10 days of their delivery; if they are not, they are returned on the next Dunkin' Donuts supply truck. Once the coffee is brewed, it can be served for only 18 minutes; after that, it must be thrown out. And the coffee must be brewed between 196 and 198 degrees Fahrenheit exactly. Dunkin' is one of the few chains that still use real cream—*not* half and half, *not* milk, *not* the sugar-based powder. No wonder the company sold 350 million cups of coffee in 1984.*

The best cup of coffee. An incredibly successful food store. The leading department store chain in the country. They all have one thing in common—extraordinary leadership. Each story includes leaders who started with a vision of the business, who shared it with others and inspired them to follow, and who fostered constant innovation and vigilance to quality in pursuit of the vision.

---

*See permission note on copyright page.

The "Unbank": The Stew Leonards of Banking

Service leaders know it is the little things that count, that keep the customers coming back. They have built the reputations of their businesses on the myriad of details that add up to service excellence. They have created organizations where it is "fun" to shop—and "fun" to work. Why not a place where it is "fun" to bank?

That was one goal of Carl J. Schmitt in 1980 when he opened University National Bank & Trust (UNB) in Palo Alto, California—and he has proved that "banking with a sense of humor" works. In 1986, UNB's return on assets was 1.02 percent and its return on equity was 14.6 percent—both well above the industry average. Not everyone can bank at UNB, however. Its targeted market is decidedly upscale, and even making a deposit requires either a thorough credit check or a strong reference from an existing customer.

Once accepted, UNB's clients suspect they might be in for an unusual banking experience when they notice the large painting on the side of the bank—an alien emerging from a space ship that has crashed into the bank wall—or the burglars, safecrackers, and counterfeiters that decorate the bank's delivery trucks. Inside, they encounter services that range from free shoeshines to an annual giveaway of Walla Walla sweet onions from a pile in the middle of the bank lobby. (Bank employees call clients to let them know when the new crop comes in.)

Schmitt's sense of humor even extends to the bank's advertising. He capitalizes on the fact the most banks claim good service, but few actually deliver it. One ad promised UNCOLA BANKING above copy that begins: "Exactly what it says. *Un*common, *un*derstated, *un*like any other bank you've ever dealt with."[9]

UNB's service extends far beyond these novelties, however. Overdrawn clients are more likely to receive a phone call than a service charge. Deposits can be made via a courier service provided by the bank. Postage stamps are sold at cost. If more than three people are waiting in line, a new teller window is opened—and often manned by a bank officer. And clients can count on their monthly statements being mailed by the second of the month; all employees are kept overtime once each month to make sure it happens.

A large part of Carl Schmitt's vision is focused on service, and the belief that most bank customers aren't getting much. With other banks, "the customer has suffered in quality of service because everybody is the same," he said. "Some people might think I'm a little hokey, but it all comes back to the 'Golden Rule.' Another way of putting it is, sit on the other side of the table and see how it feels."[10]

Like other successful service leaders, Schmitt realizes that the Golden Rule applies to employees as well as clients. UNB's employees are chosen carefully, paid at the high end of the industry scale, and believed in by management. The mindset is *not:* "We're starting to get lines out there, so you should start working faster." Rather, the orientation is: "Maybe we'd better hire another teller."[11]

Carl Schmitt formed his vision of what banking should be when, as California Superintendent of Banks (1975–78), he noted a trend toward less personalized service. He chose his market niche carefully: upscale customers in an affluent, high-tech, university town. He knows that attention to employees translates into client service. He knows how to pass his vision on to others.

"I think the best thing I can do for the bank is give it a sense of direction," he said. "I think you have to think on the long-term, which you almost never have time for, and react on the short-term in a positive way to lead your people."[10]

The lessons of high-performing service organizations in other industries are not lost on Carl Schmitt. Like Stew Leonard, Schmitt takes an entrepreneurial approach to running his business. Most other banks in Palo Alto—and most other food stores in Norwalk—no doubt look much alike, but entrepreneurs don't depend on existing role models. In many ways, they approach their businesses like they "invented" them. Their insistence on excellence starts with the fundamentals —competitive products and prices, carefully chosen, well-cared for employees—without which such details as jazz bands at the entrance or onions in the lobby are meaningless gestures. They communicate their commitment to service excellence, to excellence in general, at every opportunity. Their employees listen —and follow—because they too are caught up in the vision.

THE SERVICE LEADER'S "TOOLBOX"

The principal tool that leaders use in shaping a service-minded corporate culture—particularly if the main objective is overcoming the inertia of an existing culture to put a new one in place—is *communication*. When asked what "tools" they use to establish the importance of service in their organizations, nearly all of the executives we surveyed mention communication-related activities.

They "manage by walking around," make speeches in staff meetings, and distribute printed or videotaped newsletters. They demonstrate their commitment to service quality by their behavior, often through direct and repeated contact with customers and employees. They celebrate progress with rituals and events that foster a sense of teamwork within the organization and make heroes of employees who exemplify service standards and objectives. They listen to what employees have to say about their jobs and about their relationships with each other and their customers. And they understand that middle managers are a critical link between the executive suite and line personnel, and use them as conduits to spread the service message throughout the organization.

Service leaders never stop communicating. Jack Gilbert, Senior Vice President of First American National Bank in Tennessee, states, "Creating customer service and sales cultures . . . requires constant communication, recognition, and reinforcement. Once created, the momentum is so great that it cannot be contained. People begin to realize the only thing better than winning is winning big."

The Service Statement

One way leaders influence employees' service values is by codifying in writing the meaning and rationale of the company's service philosophy. These statements give management and employees a common language—a mutual understanding of what is expected—and establish a foundation for measuring and rewarding progress. Most importantly, they may offer an agenda around which employees can rally, a sense of purpose that financial goals alone do not instill.

One service statement we like is in use at Carteret Savings Bank in Morristown, New Jersey. Developed with broad employee participation, it says:

> Our customer is the most important person in our business.
>
> Our customer is not dependent upon us—we are dependent upon him.
>
> Our customer is not an interruption of our work—he is the purpose of it.
>
> Our customer does us a favor when he calls—we are not doing him a favor.
>
> Our customer is part of our business—not an outsider.
>
> Our customer is not a cold statistic—he is a flesh and blood human being with feelings and emotions like our own.
>
> Our customer is not someone with whom we argue or match wits.
>
> Our customer is a person who brings us his wants—it is our job to fill those wants.
>
> Our customer is deserving of the most courteous and attentive treatment we can give him.
>
> Our customer is the life-blood of our business.
>
> Our customer is the man or woman behind our paychecks—let's always remember that!
>
> THE CUSTOMER IS BOSS.

Carteret Chairman and CEO Robert B. O'Brien, Jr. states, "We let our employees know of this commitment, and constantly emphasize it by words, deeds, and in writing. Each branch has our corporate value statement framed on display. Each employee has received a paperweight reminder of our values. Each issue of our monthly employee newsletter has the value statement on its masthead."[12]

Carteret's service statement presents a set of values that are summed up by the final phrase: "The customer is boss." Saying it, of course, does not necessarily make it so, but it must be said—particularly if the emphasis on customer service is a new direction for the organization. We will discuss the complex task of establishing specific, measurable service standards in a later chapter. But that task is helped with the development of a written, widely distributed definition of the institution's service philosophy.

Verbal Reinforcement and Personal Example

No matter how well crafted the written service statement, it is destined to become an empty message without continuing personal reinforcement of it from organizational leaders. Leaders understand that an organization's written words can gain or lose meaning depending on the manner and extent to which they reflect those words in their own behavior. Only by constantly demonstrating their own commitment to service excellence do service leaders influence the attitudes and actions of their subordinates. For this reason, successful service leaders underline the importance of service at virtually every opportunity. "Just about every senior management talk to the staff includes some reference to the importance of service quality," says a senior executive of a west coast bank. "Our CEO uses airlines as an example of a 'deregulated' industry that has done it—for the most part—wrong."

At Richmond Savings in Vancouver, Canada, the modes of communication include "constant, regular, and informal discussions coupled with written communications to all levels of staff stressing the value of service quality, often including specific examples and their positive impact on the organization," according to President and CEO Donald F. Tuline. In addition, weekly senior management meetings have an open agenda for discussing projects and sharing ideas involving service quality. Tuline says that this approach fosters "a search for the truth" by the group, rather than "a forum to earn personal points."

"My most important tool is striving to set a high standard and example of personal behavior and professional performance," says John G. Medlin, Jr., Chairman, President, and CEO of First Wachovia Corporation. "I constantly emphasize service quality through written and oral communication to managers, employees, and trainees. I personally respond to letters from customers about our services or people, and require that complaints be handled the day received. We make a special effort to provide positive reinforcement by commending employees for quality service. In general, I try to create an attitude and atmosphere in which quality service is a routine way of life."

Stanley J. Calderon, President and CEO of Bank One in Lafayette, Indiana, states, "It is not uncommon for me to interrupt any particular function to answer a customer's call. I stop by our branch offices frequently to thank our staff for their efforts toward improving quality, and to chat with customers."

Adds Alexander Berry, III, Senior Executive Vice President of Signet Bank/Virginia, "To reinforce service quality, I attempt to lead by example, to reward publicly those who provide quality service, to speak to the issue whenever I have the opportunity, to have service quality as a goal for all my managers even though it is hard to measure, to constantly relate service and sales as inseparable, to constantly ask the question whenever we make a decision: 'How will this affect our customers?'"

Leaders understand that establishing a service-minded culture in their organizations requires more than lip service. By demonstrating their personal commitment every day, by addressing the issue at every opportunity, they encourage others in the organization to make service quality part of their daily routines as well. Leaders personally interact with employees and customers to carry the service message, to listen, and to identify problems. They personally commend employees who best reflect the institution's service philosophy. They understand that they are the prime movers, that verbal communication is the richest form of communication, and that personal involvement is the richest form of endorsement. As one senior executive from a large institution comments, "Only an act of God could stop me from being this way."

Rituals and Events

Peters and Waterman call it "hoopla and razzle dazzle."[13] What they are referring to is the sense of celebration and the use of events and rituals that characterize successful "people-oriented" corporate cultures. In making their point, they quote author William Manchester, who in describing his World War II experiences, observed, "A man wouldn't sell his life to you, but he will give it to you for a piece of colored ribbon."[14]

Berry and Rieder refer to rituals and events as "parades." They write:[15]

> For service workers, the potential for being defeated by the rigors and grind of the job and for allowing customers to become nameless, faceless "flatties" is ever present.
>
> Service quality parades—big extravaganzas planned months in advance as well as small, impromptu "miniparades"—can recharge service workers' batteries, lift their spirits, and prevent mental "brownouts."
>
> These events give meaning to the routine, even drudgery, of service work. They give tangible, visible recognition to superior performers, while spurring at least some of the "also-rans" to get with the program.

Security Pacific National Bank uses several rituals in its Circle of Excellence Awards program, for which winners are nominated by branch personnel and approved both by their immediate supervisors and a judging committee at bank headquarters. One is an annual awards dinner for the approximately 300 winners statewide. The other is a "surprise" night out, celebrated when the award is first announced in the branch, complete with a speech from the winner's supervisor and a standing ovation from other branch employees. Winners also achieve special status within the bank. Former Executive Vice President Nick Baker says, "They then become part of our 'unofficial input' on customer service, and their recommendations are taken very seriously. They can write to us saying, 'I'm a Circle of Excellence winner. Have you thought of doing this?' As a result of this program, we've made literally hundreds of small changes to make things easier for our customers."

The use of rituals and events is particularly important in organizations undergoing a culture change. They emphasize to all employees that behaviors which support the new cultural direction are beneficial not only to the organization, but to themselves. In addition, they give senior management opportunities to visibly throw their support behind service quality.

Creating Middle Management Service Leadership

Superior service quality requires inspired leadership at all levels of the organization, not just at the top. Thus, a key leadership challenge for senior executives is reaching middle managers with the service quality mandate, and creating an organizational environment that encourages them to be leaders, too. As we stressed in Chapter 3, middle managers are the people in the organization for whom almost all other employees work. The presence or absence of their leadership will be a critical factor in the service quality journey.

Many middle managers in financial services come from financial and technical backgrounds. They often think in terms of facts, processes, and procedures, and are used to being measured on such criteria as productivity, chargeoffs, fees, and profits. These managers frequently have difficulty in relating to service quality, perceiving it to be a "mushy" concept. G. Lynn Shostack, Chairman and President of Joyce International states, "I don't think anyone is resistant to the *idea* that service quality is important. But many are legitimately cynical about all the talk, 'touchy-feely' programs, and 'motivational' claptrap they've seen or been forced to participate in that has had no demonstrable results."

One tool at the disposal of senior executives is to regularly bring middle managers together to discuss service quality. Middle managers are more likely to accept service quality's importance if the subject is given high priority at meetings and if a special effort is made to position service quality as definable, measurable, and profitable. Service discussions at these meetings can include: the institution's service priorities and programs, marketing research on customer service expectations and perceptions, data on customer complaints and the costs of poor quality, and quality improvement ideas that come from the field. Middle managers are most likely to become supportive and involved if they are included in program planning, progress reviews, and any sharing of ideas and information.

Senior executives can also encourage middle managers to experiment more on behalf of improving service quality. Financial institution employees are often burdened with restrictive procedures and policies that hamper initiative and exacerbate service problems that might otherwise be easily solved. Middle managers are in the position to encourage service providers to use their judgment in serving customers. Service rigidity and quality service often are incompatible. If service providers believe that their jobs are on the line if they make mistakes or deviate ever so slightly from policies, they will become rigid in the service role, frustrating or angering their customers. One bank executive interviewed recalled an incident in which a teller, reacting to instructions not to execute further transactions with an overdrawn customer, called the manager to see if it would be all right to accept a deposit!

In some cases, a solution can be found by realizing that across-the-board procedures and regulations do not always fit branches facing different market conditions. National Bank of Detroit is attempting to solve this problem with its "Think Project," in which the staff at three pilot branches were told, "You are closest to your customers and in the best position to determine how to serve them. You cannot throw out the rule book, but you can change it to improve service. Run the branch as though it was your own business."

As a result of this program, personnel in the participating branches discovered that little things can make a big impression on customers. One branch located near housing for senior citizens began accepting senior citizen ID cards as one of two pieces of required identification for transactions. Another branch began cashing checks for noncustomers at drive-in windows as a way to build cross-selling opportunities. Another relaxed the customary "hold" policy on third-party checks when customers were known. Each of these changes ran counter to existing bank policy. During the pilot period, branches were not held responsible for losses—but no losses occurred. The success of the program has led National Bank of Detroit to implement it across the branch system.[16]

Middle managers are the crucial link between top management and customer contact and operations personnel. It is essential that middle managers reinforce and build on the service quality message coming from the top of the organization; it is essential that middle managers become service leaders, too.

CONVERTING THE SKEPTICS

Middle managers are not the only ones who may need convincing that service quality is a top priority—and that a cultural change is necessary to embark on the journey toward improved service. The financial services industry is still adjusting to deregulation, and one of the major adjustments involves personnel at all levels, including senior managers, who have not yet accepted the new realities of sales and service.

In short, most financial institutions employ skeptics who will need to be converted to the customer service philosophy. Even people who admit that it is no longer "business as usual" may have difficulty changing long-entrenched viewpoints and established ways of doing things. It can be a tricky situation, because it doesn't work if the skeptics merely *say* they have seen the light. They have to really be converted.

One way to turn nonbelievers into believers is to *show them* the value of service excellence. William M. Fackler, Executive Vice President of Barnett Banks in Jacksonville, Florida, says, "In an organization like Barnett, made up of individual autonomous units, we have the advantage of seeing success in one bank become a role model for others. Banks, like other organizations, emulate successful operations. Ultimately, they have to come to the empirical conclusion that quality service is the 'secret' of success, the differential advantage, the 'value added.' In the final analysis, though, everyone—believers and nonbelievers—will rise or fall to the level of quality service expectations set by their corporate culture."

Fackler makes two important points. The first is familiar: an organization's culture unleashes or restricts the possibilities for service excellence. The second is often overlooked: success breeds success. The surest way to convert nonbelievers is to prove through pilot projects in selected branches or departments that improved service quality can result in happier customers, more motivated employees, and a more profitable bottom line.

Consultant George Rieder recommends the power of self-discovery. He states, "The process of discovery is strong stuff, so let doubters reflect on their own treatment as consumers. Have them list the service turn-ons and turn-offs they have experienced personally. Have them relate stories from friends and bank customers concerning service quality at financial institutions. Horror stories surface quickly. So do accounts of individuals going the proverbial second mile to give not only service, but of themselves. Between the two extremes, doubters will see the no man's land of undistinguished, banal service ripe for the pickings by high-performing institutions."

Others we surveyed say their conversion techniques include:

- "Getting people personally involved in the resolution of a service problem that helps keep a customer, then translating what that means into long-term revenue for us."
- "Developing success stories that show proof of the value of service quality."
- "Rewarding—frequently and publicly—those who deliver quality."
- "Training. In all of our training modules—from executive development to very technical training for clerical staff—we spend time on the subject of quality customer service and its importance to the bank."
- "Enrolling—and re-enrolling—employees in quality service training programs."

- "Reversing roles by putting employees in the customer's role during training."

When it comes to converting skeptics who don't yet believe in the competitive necessity of top-level service quality, the financial institutions we studied use a number of common techniques. One of the most effective is demonstrating that quality service is a profit strategy through educational and training programs and pilot projects that establish empirically the bottom-line impact of improved service. Another technique that works is establishing measurable standards as the basis for recognition and reward programs; extra money in the pocket will get the attention of at least some hard core nonbelievers.

However, the most common conversion technique—once again—is personal leadership. By making their commitment to service quality clear, by having a service vision and communicating it constantly, service leaders say in effect, "This is the way it is. If you don't like it, there is no place for you here!"

MAKE THE PERSONAL COMMITMENT

The service quality journey begins with a leadership decision —the decision that such a journey is the key for the growth, profitability, and perhaps the very existence of the organization. Leadership that is personal, emphatic, and relentless is necessary to overcome the inertia of existing culture, chart the new direction, and keep the travelers on their course.

We agree with Carteret Chairman and CEO, Robert B. O'Brien, Jr., who says, "Senior management commitment is essential. We are the vital example to everyone in the bank. We make the personal commitment to service. We support the efforts of those within the bank who provide service to our customers."

Service quality, leadership, and communication are inseparable. Leadership is the cornerstone of a service-minded culture, and communication is the cornerstone of leadership. Managership in and of itself is insufficient. To those who are prepared to assume the mantle of leadership for service quality, we conclude by saying:

> Belief in the ability to provide superior service is a vision. Take the vision as your own. Believe in it. Support it. Develop standards for what constitutes service excellence in your organization, and communicate them. Work with both managers and others to educate them about service quality. Show them that service is a profit strategy. Share your vision unceasingly. Demonstrate your belief in the vision through your own actions, and know that by doing so, you will influence others as well. It won't be easy. And certainly, believing in and supporting the vision is not the whole answer. You will also need research to find out where you are; training to get where you want to go; job descriptions that reflect new responsibilities; incentive and reward systems that support progress; perhaps even a new organizational structure to encourage the growth of a service culture. But the vision is essential. The vision is the first step of the journey.

NOTES

1. Hoffman, Gail. "Quality Service Can Be Achieved If Commitment Starts at the Top." *American Banker,* October 13, 1987, p. 17.
2. Conner, Daryl R., Byron G. Fiman, and Ernest E. Clements. "Corporate Culture and Its Impact on Strategic Change in Banking." *Journal of Retail Banking,* Summer 1987, p. 17.
3. Peters, Thomas J. *Thriving on Chaos.* New York, NY: Alfred A. Knopf, Inc., 1987, pp. 3–4.
4. Bennis, Warren, and Burt Nanus. *Leaders: The Strategies for Taking Charge,* New York, NY: Harper & Row, 1985.
5. Clifford, Donald K., and Richard E. Cavanaugh. *The Winning Performance: How America's High-Growth Midsize Companies Succeed,* New York, NY: Bantam Books, 1985, p. 78.
6. Peters, Thomas J., and Nancy Austin. *A Passion for Excellence.* New York, NY: Random House, 1985.
7. Clifford, Donald K., and Richard E. Cavanagh. *The Winning Performance: How America's High-Growth Midsize Companies Succeed.* New York, NY: Bantam Books, 1985, p. 16.
8. Ibid, p. 66.

9. Hawken, Paul. *Growing a Business.* New York, NY: Simon and Schuster, 1987, p. 177.
10. Brouillette, Geoff. "Service with a Smirk." *The California Executive,* November 1987, p. 37.
11. Ibid, p. 36.
12. O'Brien, Robert B., Jr. "Customer Concern as the Key to High Performance." Speech presented to Financial Institutions Marketing Association Mid-Year Conference, Colorado Springs, Colorado, July 1987.
13. Peters, Thomas J., and Robert H. Waterman. *In Search of Excellence,* New York, NY: Harper & Row, 1982, p. 241.
14. Ibid, p. 268.
15. Berry, Leonard L., and George A. Rieder. "Parade Is Festive Way to Honor Service Workers." *American Banker,* December 31, 1987, p. 4.
16. Berry, Leonard L. "Include Middle Managers in the Quest for Quality." *American Banker,* September 23, 1987.

PART 2

SERVICE QUALITY—BEYOND COMMITMENT

CHAPTER 6

SETTING THE SERVICE
QUALITY AGENDA

When our service quality program started two years ago, the initial focus was looking at things from the customers' point of view, and the only way to understand the customers' point of view is to go out and ask them.
—Gary McCuen, Vice President and
Manager of Corporate Service Quality, Bank of America

Financial services executives who accept the challenge of service leadership are apt to find themselves struggling at a crossroads, fighting to change the direction of an organization that is well on its way down a road marked "operations cost-efficiency." In most financial institutions, much of what happens at the point of customer contact is driven by the objective of cost-containment, which may undermine the objective of high quality service delivery. The trick is in balancing the two, in steering the organization down a middle road that combines operational efficiency with the highest quality service the institution can muster.

It won't be easy, and it won't be a "quick fix." As Richard Davis, Senior Vice President and Manager of Customer Service Administration for Security Pacific National Bank, comments, "We're not a company that's brand new to the market. We're more than 100 years old, and we have a reputation that's not going to change overnight. But if you don't put a stake in the ground and start to move it, you're not going to get anywhere. The second thing to remember is that your reputation—be it good or bad—is powerful and you must respect that power. You can't change things that quickly, and if you're not careful, you might end up making a long-range impression you don't want."

To embark on the service quality journey you have to start somewhere, and you have to give that start careful consideration. But how and where? Like any journey, this one begins with determining where you are, deciding where you want to go, then mapping a route—an action plan—that will enable you to find your way. Fortunately, there are some guidelines to help you. One of the most important is to remember that service quality improvement is not just a case of "fixing" 2 or 3 big things and making them 50 percent better; it is also taking 100 little things and making them 10 percent better.

Another critical point to remember is that service excellence should be established throughout the organization as an ongoing effort, a real and permanent change. Security Pacific's Davis states, "My advice to other senior executives is: don't play a game with service quality. Don't create a program out of it, because that in itself is implicitly short-term. Create a focus, but don't even talk about it until you're ready to do something. The worst thing that can happen is to let it fall on deaf ears or to announce you're going to have a focus on the customer. 'The Year of the Customer!' That's ludicrous! What's next year going to be?"

We have already emphasized the importance of management commitment, but what does that commitment include? It is certainly more than a commitment of resources. In fact, service quality improvement does not necessarily mean a huge monetary investment. More important is a commitment of management time—time to talk, share, agree on what the organization's values are, identify roadblocks, and jointly determine how problems can be solved. That happens over time, layer by layer, up and down the organization, until people throughout the organization are singing the same tune, vibrating with the same frequency. Priorities have to be set. Management has to decide what to do and what not to do, then find —or develop—internal sponsors to act on those priorities.

"After senior management buy-in, make it clear to the bank how important management thinks service quality is," one bank consultant warns. "We are currently working with a bank where there is support at the top, but where communication is poor. The message has not gotten down strongly to the next level. That makes implementation difficult because area and branch managers have not heard a lot about service quality from the senior people, and are not as responsive as they might otherwise be to service improvement efforts—either training or systems and facilities changes."

The impetus for service improvement may start at the top, but service quality happens at the grass roots. People close to the customer need to be empowered, to be brought into the loop, and given some say in the strategies and ideas necessary to measure and improve service in their own areas. In the words of Robert DiAlexandris, Senior Vice President, National Bank of Detroit, "The role of leadership is to determine the thrust, to communicate and persuade, to begin the momentum—and then to get out of the way. The tactics of implementation must be left to individual business units."

TAKING ACTION: THE JOURNEY BEGINS

There is no one "map," no single agenda, that can guide all financial institutions down the road marked "service excellence." Different institutions have different cultures, different markets—and different service problems that require unique solutions. There are, however, a number of essentials that must be in place or the journey will be nearly impossible to make. Visionary, committed leaders who understand the power and importance of communication are one essential.

Another essential is information. Visionary, committed leaders armed with relevant information weaken the "Service Wall"—the existing culture that is blocking service excellence. Knocking down this formidable barrier involves identifying customer service desires and perceptions. It also requires isolating the roadblocks that stand in the way of quality service, categorizing them by importance, and then finding ways to remove them within the constraints of available resources and according to the overall goals of the organization.

The journey, then, begins with service leaders armed with information about what customers want, what they perceive they are getting, and what roadblocks are standing in the way. The journey begins with understanding the service quality gap (Gap 5), then creating an agenda for closing it.

RESEARCH OFFERS DOSES OF REALITY

"When it comes to quality service, most banks don't know how much trouble they are in," a leading bank consultant comments. Furthermore, many of them don't know how to find out. The reason, of course, is that service quality is such an elusive concept. Yet determining ways to measure service quality is essential not only for identifying customer desires and solving problems, but also for developing service performance standards and rewarding employees who exceed them.

John M. Davis, President and CEO of Fidelity State Bank in Garden City, Kansas sums up the problem when he says, "Since our definition of quality service requires conformance to a standard, the measurement of individual performance and bank performance against the established standards is necessary."

The use of research to pave the way for service improvement is critical at any stage of the service quality journey. At the beginning of the journey—a time when many decisions have to be made and a road map prepared—credible, consistent information from a number of sources is invaluable. As an early step in the cultural change process, research often provides hard, objective data that service performance is not as good as management thinks it is. Thus, research can provide just the dose of reality needed to overcome the twin villains of complacency and inertia while simultaneously indicating what needs to be changed and in what order of priority. Once the journey is underway, ongoing service quality research enables management to track progress, monitor shifts in both employee performance and customer expectations, and evaluate the impact of internal developments ranging from new training programs to key personnel changes.

The possibilities are many, including: customer and noncustomer surveys that probe service expectations and perceptions, employee surveys, "tone of service" surveys, "shopper" research, and careful monitoring and management of customer complaints. We strongly recommend using most or all of these methods to measure service quality. Using multiple research approaches compensates for the limitations of any one methodology and offers richer insight into what is really going on—and why.[1]

Gap 1 Revisited

Senior management often has definite ideas about what customers value most in terms of service and typically will use these ideas to establish the goals, policies, and offerings that set the service tone for the organization. Unfortunately, senior management is often wrong in its assumptions about customers.

The problem here is Gap 1—the discrepancy between what customers want from the service and what management thinks they want. Executives who are isolated from daily contact with customers are especially vulnerable to Gap 1 mistakes.

We recommend that senior executives put themselves in direct customer contact on an ongoing basis. Policy-makers need to talk to customers standing in line and when they open or close accounts. They need to telephone new and experienced customers each week and ask how the institution can improve its service performance. They need to gather some primary data that is not filtered through a survey in order to gain a first-hand sense of what needs to be done.

In addition to the information gained, a visible interest in what customers think of the service being offered can go a long way toward convincing employees that top management is serious about improving service quality. At The Royal Bank of Canada, anyone from the president of the bank to senior regional managers and vice presidents might appear unannounced at a branch, ready to roll up their sleeves and go to work.

Quality of Service Manager Keith Oosthoek explains, "If a branch is short-staffed on a given day, all it takes is a call downtown to have a member of what's called the 'Brass Brigade' come out to do whatever is necessary. In the process, they talk to customers and so become familiar with their concerns, and also show employees that the people downtown are really aware of what they go through in a day."

At a Royal Bank branch in Ottawa, managers call clients daily and conduct a 5-minute interview to see if they are getting the service they require. "Ninety-nine percent of the comments are positive, and we take the opportunity to reinforce our relationship with the client," Oosthoek says. "If there is a problem, we try to resolve it right away. In other branches, managers get that feedback by walking the line and talking to customers as they are being serviced. A good manager always has his eyes and ears wide open for customers' reactions."

Management's interaction with customers is an effective way to begin closing Gap 1, but it is insufficient in and of itself. More formal research—with customers and employees alike—is needed to close Gap 1 and, in general, help an organization deliver a level of service consistent with customer expectations.

Expectation and Perception Surveys

An imperative in service quality research is measuring both service expectations and perceptions, since customer service desires shape perceptions of what actually transpires. One tool for measuring the level of service quality is SERVQUAL, a multiple-item instrument developed and validated by Parasuraman, Zeithaml, and Berry.[2] Based on the notion of "perceived quality," SERVQUAL is a quantitative yardstick that measures customers' perceptions of service performance against the backdrop of their expectations (or desires) for the service. The expectation and perception statements in SERVQUAL fit the five dimensions of service quality introduced in Chapter 2, namely, tangibles, reliability, responsiveness, assurance, and empathy. Both expectation and perception scores are measured on seven-point scales, from "strongly agree" to "strongly disagree." Overall service quality scores are the differences between the perception and expectation scores. (See Figure 6–1 for several examples of SERVQUAL items.)

Using SERVQUAL, financial institutions can assess their service performance along each of the five dimensions, as well as determine their overall level of service quality by averaging scores across all five dimensions. Individual branches with sim-

FIGURE 6–1

SERVQUAL Compares Customers' Service Expectations with Perceptions

	Strongly Agree	*Strongly Disagree*
Examples of Expectation Statements		
The physical facilities of banks should be visually appealing.	7 6 5 4 3 2 1	
When banks promise to do something by a certain time, they should do so.	7 6 5 4 3 2 1	
When customers have problems, banks should be sympathetic and reassuring.	7 6 5 4 3 2 1	
It is unrealistic to expect employees to know what the needs of their customers are.	7 6 5 4 3 2 1	
Examples of Perception Statements		
XYZ Bank's physical facilities are visually appealing.	7 6 5 4 3 2 1	
When XYZ Bank promises to do something by a certain time, it does it.	7 6 5 4 3 2 1	
When you have problems, XYZ Bank is sympathetic and reassuring.	7 6 5 4 3 2 1	
Employees of XYZ Bank do not know what your needs are.	7 6 5 4 3 2 1	

The difference between the ratings on pairs of statements like these is a measure of perceived service quality. The *higher* (more positive) the perception-minus-expectation score, the *higher* the level of perceived service quality.

Source: Parasuraman A., Zeithaml Valarie and Berry Leonard L. *SERVQUAL: A Multiple-Item Scale for Measuring Customer Perceptions of Service Quality.* Cambridge, Mass.: Marketing Science Institute, 1986.

ilar scores can be grouped into clusters, enabling management to study the key factors that facilitate or hinder the delivery of high quality service.

In addition, the separate examination of expectations and perceptions makes SERVQUAL a convenient instrument for measuring the service quality of competing organizations. In surveys that encompass competitors, respondents need only to be asked to identify and then rate their primary institution on the perception questions. Periodic market-wide surveys enable an institution to compare its service with that of the competition and to identify salient service dimensions in which competitors may have an edge.[3]

As a diagnostic tool, SERVQUAL can clarify service desires (based on expectation scores), identify the service dimensions on which the institution is weakest (based on perception scores), and isolate the areas having the largest expectation/perception gaps (based on perception-minus-expectation scores).

One valuable question to ask is whether the respondent would recommend the institution to a friend. Whereas 75 percent of the respondents in a survey may claim to be "satisfied" with the service organization, only 50 percent may be willing to recommend it. Customers need to be very pleased with a company before they will recommend it to friends. Thus, monitoring the percentage of customers willing to recommend the institution is one of the best overall barometers of customer service impressions available.[4]

SERVQUAL is often administered as a mail questionnaire. Other alternatives exist, however. One bank we studied distributes a set of five questionnaires in its branches—one for each day of the week. Each questionnaire concerns one of the five service quality dimensions, providing the user with a sampling of that week's customers. SERVQUAL also can be administered in the form of telephone or face-to-face interviews.

SERVQUAL would normally be administered two to four times a year. A single application of expectations/perceptions research offers a still picture of service quality at a given point in time. However, quality is a moving target and must be tracked over time. Expectations change. Perceptions change.

The only way to measure service quality is to do it on an ongoing basis.

For Gail George, Vice President of Training and Development at Perpetual Savings Bank, Alexandria, Virginia, results of SERVQUAL research offered several surprises. "Customers rated the service they receive higher than we would have thought, which came as a welcome surprise," she says. "Our customers rated our service the same as did the customers of other banks, but because our customers had higher expectations, the size of the gaps between the service they expected and the service they perceived they were getting was greater than for the competition—not a situation we were happy about. The biggest surprise, however, was that our managers and staff rated us so much lower than our customers did, so we were not giving ourselves enough credit."

The study's focus on customer expectations, George adds, has resulted in "a real shift in the way we look at standards. We realized that we need to be measuring service using customer expectations rather than internal productivity measures. Many of our standards, for example, were set based on history—average availability of the ATM network became the measure of 'reliability.' We measured success as plus or minus the standard. Now we must set and meet standards that keep customers satisfied—that focus on what customers are getting rather than simply what we are giving. That's a real shift in our thinking."

SERVQUAL in Action: Security Pacific National Bank

"You have to have a senior management that says, 'Okay, you go out and tell us what people think of us, and we'll do something with it.' Security Pacific National Bank, to my knowledge, had never before asked a large group of people what they thought about our service," says Richard Davis. "The worst thing we could have done was to ask and not do anything about it. So if you do ask, listen and act. Otherwise, forget it! If the feedback had said we were wonderful, we wouldn't need it. If our mission statement had said that we only wanted to be as good as everybody else, we wouldn't need it either. But our mission statement says we want to be better than the rest, and we want to do it to drive profit. We believe that. And the data say, 'You're only the same. You're not there yet.' "

The data to which Davis refers was generated from SERV-QUAL research, which is the basis for the bank's efforts to define and improve customer service. Questionnaires were sent to a representative sample of the market, asking customers to assess both Security Pacific Bank and its major competitors on the five dimensions of service quality. The results showed that the bank was falling below customer expectations, but more so in some areas than others—less in regard to tangibles, for example, but more in the area of empathy. That, according to Davis, indicated where the emphasis—and money—for corrective action could best be placed.

"The philosophy of the process is to use a randomly selected scoring mechanism providing tangible results that can be translated back into behavior modification. If you don't, I assure you that you'll get nobody's attention," Davis says. "And if we left it to individual discretion, we'd continue to operate the way we are. Understanding is coming at the hard cost of a lot of time and discussion."

Much of the time spent is Davis' time, and the discussion includes one-on-one visits with almost every manager in the bank. Davis states, "I've found that the words mean nothing until I've translated them into further dimensions that relate to the individual receiving them. For example, when we define 'reliability' in terms of its service impact for Security Pacific Bank specifically, one of the things we come up with is that customers deserve and expect the same level of service and information at every banking office within our system. In fact, when we discuss the service impact for each of the five dimensions, we always start with the words 'customers deserve and expect.' "

"My goal during the meetings with individual managers is to take down their defenses about issues that bother them, but also to get them to say, 'I know all that!' And the answer is, 'Yes, you do! You know what I know, but you haven't categorized it in the thought processes that I have. You need to know how to use that information. You are the only person who can empower your banking office to change—not me, not the regional vice president, but you, the manager. And until you understand this, your people aren't going to believe it and empower it to the level it needs to be.' "

Security Pacific National Bank's focus on service quality is centered on the idea that each of the bank's customers expects and deserves the same level of service. To the statement, "Gee, Richard, the expectations of customers here in Beverly Hills are different from customers in Fresno," Davis answers, "That's not true!" The emphasis may be a bit different, but in the defined areas of tangibles, reliability, responsiveness, assurance, and empathy, demographic breakdowns of the SERVQUAL research show that expectations are the same everywhere.

"We're not talking about minimum expectations here," Davis adds. "We're talking about exceeding our existing expectations goal. If you start thinking minimum, you'll get minimum. And I can't afford that!"

Employee Surveys

Research efforts should not concentrate on customers alone. No one is more aware of internal roadblocks to service than employees. All employees provide a service of one kind or another, and they know what is getting in the way of improved service in the institution. Also, customer contact people who are on the firing line day after day can discuss service problems from a different perspective than customers. While customers may report that service is poor and that contact personnel appear unwilling or unable to please customers, employees often know the causes of the problem—the "whys" behind service shortfalls.

As "customers" of various internal support services, employees are in an ideal position to evaluate the quality of these intermediate services. If an organization is serious about improving service quality, meeting the service expectations of internal customers is every bit as important as meeting the expectations of external customers. Poor internal service lowers employee productivity and morale and raises service delivery costs. And inadequate internal support of service providers will surely translate into unsatisfactory service from the customer's perspective.

Like customer research, employee research should be ongoing in order to track shifting expectations and perceptions. Among other questions, we recommend including the following in employee service quality surveys:[5]

- What is your biggest day-to-day problem in trying to provide good service?
- If you were president of the bank and could make only one change to improve service quality, what change would you make?

Our experience is that these two questions are extremely powerful. If employee respondents have even a modicum of faith in management, and if they are promised anonymity in their responses, they will answer these two questions with a degree of insight and realism available from no other source.

One of the major problems top management faces in improving service quality is communicating—and reinforcing—the service message downward through the organization. Tracking what employees think of service, both internally and at the customer level, and removing obstacles impeding service will reinforce the message that management thinks service counts!

Individual Performance Tracking

Service quality stems from an accumulation of individual employee performances. Accordingly, it is essential to measure service performance at the individual employee level in addition to measuring institutional performance through instruments like SERVQUAL. Two approaches for tracking individual employee performance are "tone of service" surveys and shopper research.

Tone of service research involves systematically monitoring customer perceptions following service encounters. The idea is to capture service impressions while they are still fresh. For example, a sample of customers opening new accounts could be immediately sent a questionnaire with a series of "yes or no" questions about the helpfulness, courtesy, and competence of the service representative. Since the name of the employee opening the account is known, it is possible to periodically provide individual employees with their tone of service scores and to factor these data into the performance appraisal process.

Friendly Bank in Oklahoma City asks the following questions in its new accounts tone of service survey:

1. How long did you have to wait?
2. On your arrival, did our representative identify himself/herself?
3. Was the representative knowledgeable about the services offered to you?
4. Did our representative provide you with sufficient information about our services?
5. If you opened a checking account, was our "Hold Policy" explained to you?
6. Were you satisfied with the length of time required to open your account?
7. At the conclusion of the visit, did the representative thank you by name?
8. In summary, did you feel:
   —Our representative helped you in a very pleasant and professional manner?
   —Our representative did just what was expected, went through the motions?
   —Our representative was not very helpful . . . you felt turned off?
9. Please feel free to tell us how we might improve.

A similar survey is used for customers who apply for loans. Friendly Bank's President, Jim Daniel, explains, "Questionnaires are sent to one of every five customers, including those who have been turned down for loans. Regular surveys allow us to find out if our service quality training systems are 'taking' and to track people or branches who deviate from the norm. They are also valuable for generating leads. For example, we ask them if they would like additional information on IRAs or other products. The sales we make this way more than pay for the cost of the surveys."

The use of "shoppers"—researchers who pose as customers to evaluate the performance of service providers—is a useful alternative or supplement for tone of service surveys. The researchers use a rating form to facilitate systematic and comprehensive evaluations. "Shopper" research is useful as a tool for measuring and rewarding individual service behavior and for identifying employees who may need additional coaching or training in service skills. Moreover, aggregated shopper data reveal the specific performance dimensions in which service delivery is breaking down.

Shopper research need not be a turn-off for employees. One key is to use the approach positively and constructively as a basis for recognizing outstanding service providers and for helping those who receive lower scores. Another key is to be candid with employees, making it clear that they will be "shopped" from time to time. A third key is shopping service providers several times during a performance appraisal period to minimize the potential bias of just one measurement encounter.[6]

Complaint Solicitation and Analysis

Conducting research to find out what customers and employees expect from service providers, and what they perceive the service to be, is a new step for many financial institutions. All institutions, however, already have some experience with customer complaints. Customer complaints can be a very useful form of feedback, especially if a formal process is established for soliciting, tracking, and responding to them.

As one bank executive we surveyed comments, "It is my observation that customer complaints offer rare opportunities to deliver quality service, since it is only when a customer is willing to communicate with the bank and register a complaint that we can really do something about correcting the situation which caused the customer's concern in the first place."

Another bank executive we interviewed agrees that the monitoring of complaints is very important and very cheap feedback and research. "Every complaint that comes into the district or head office is entered in the computer. Whenever we see one category that jumps out at us, we immediately try to make some positive changes so we don't alienate the many other customers who don't bother to write and just walk away."

Effective complaint research involves making it easy for customers to register a complaint and encouraging them to do so. Possible complaint mechanisms include well-promoted customer service telephone lines, preaddressed postage-paid cards or forms readily available in service facilities, and feedback forms mailed with statements.

Also important are categorizing and monitoring data, looking for trends (that is, specific types of complaints that are becoming more or less prominent). Categorizing and tracking complaints help to identify problems in the service system that require immediate attention.

Methods of responding to complaints vary, but many financial institutions find that personal attention from top management is most effective. "At United Bank of Denver, complaints and compliments alike enter the bank in four ways: through the president's office, my office, via division managers, or through employees themselves," comments Beverly Haddon, Executive Vice President. "We then compile them into a monthly report and look at the information, both quantitatively and qualitatively. Complaints are handled through the president's office or through my office because that's the way the customer wants it. They want top management to address the problem."

Illustrating this latter point is a story an executive from another bank tells of a letter he received from a customer who had experienced "long delays, general incompetence, and rudeness" at one of the bank's branches. "The letter was almost apologetic in tone, but it was obvious that the situation had existed for some time and that the customer had experienced this less than satisfactory service for more than 6 months. His response when I placed a personal call to his office to apologize for the unsatisfactory experience was one of absolute amazement. He said that no one from a bank had ever called him before, nor had he ever received a communication expressing appreciation for the multiservice relationship he had developed with our bank over the years."

Three months after the letter had been received and appropriate corrective action taken, the bank executive and the administrator of the branch in question invited the customer to lunch. At the luncheon, the customer reported an absolute 180-degree turnaround in terms of performance and service.

"As a final step, we followed up with another phone call 6 months after the luncheon to be certain he was still experiencing the level of service he expected and deserved from our organization," the executive says. "We have since had several new customers who have attributed their decision to open accounts with us to this situation and how we handled the complaint."

Institutionalizing a proactive, continuous complaint management system is far more important than commonly thought. Without such a system, an institution is destined to ignore certain policies, practices, and people that are unnecessarily damaging its service reputation.[7]

SETTING SERVICE STANDARDS

Once the appropriate research data have been compiled and analyzed, the sponsoring organization is in a position to develop service standards based on what customers expect in the service encounter. These standards must be: expressed in active measurable terms; complete, with clear objective indicators of performance; and achievable with given resources.

Another way of looking at the standard-setting process is that standards should answer the questions "What?" and "How often?" "What" specifies the required service behavior, and "How often" refers to the frequency with which it is expected.

For example, the "What" of a service standard might specify that new accounts representatives should follow-up on initial information obtained from customers, with further questions aimed at determining optimum solutions, including the need for additional services. Other standards might include referring to the customer by name, offering the customer undivided attention, and thanking the customer. In this situation, the answer to "How often" would be "in every customer interaction."

Well-conceived service standards will reflect the customer

service expectations that research has identified as important. Indeed, the standard-setting process is really a matter of defining customer service expectations in a way that service personnel fully understand them. As such, service standards help clarify work roles, communicate organizational priorities, and provide benchmarks for performance evaluation.

Service standards should not be complex or numerous. If service standards are complex, they will not be sufficiently clear. If there are many standards, they will not be sufficiently valued. Importantly, service standards should always be developed with the input of the employees they will affect. Sometimes this process may include employees from more than one department. In Bank of America, service standards were developed simultaneously for a group of corporate banking departments. The standards were based on research indicating that clients' top service concerns were timeliness, accuracy, and responsiveness.

"When we began setting standards, we found that we needed some internal standards and measures that supported the end-to-end external standards," explains Gary McCuen, Vice President and Manager of Corporate Service Quality. "There might be three or four processing steps in each transaction, so each contributing department needed to be in on the goal-setting process for each procedure. Customers don't care about how many steps you have to go through. They only care about the final result."

The process of setting standards became a "real meeting of the minds," according to McCuen. "We discussed the various interaction points, then asked the participants to pretend they were customers and decide what their expectations would be. Usually, the result was 100 percent accuracy within a given timeframe. For example, Account Reconcilement had been performing one certain procedure in 10 days with 98 percent accuracy. Now, they are down to 5 days with 100 percent accuracy. Another department head is trying to beat the expectation set for her department. The goal was set at an industry average of 2.8 errors per 10,000 transactions. She is working to drive the error rate down to 2.0."

Negotiating service performance standards with employees helps ensure that the final standards are credible, achievable, and worthwhile. Most important is the sense of involvement that results, the feeling that "We are all in this together." Improving service quality stops being a vague mandate from top management, and becomes something that employees are part of, understand, are challenged by, and believe in. This is especially so when individual performance is measured against the standards and outstanding performance is rewarded (subjects we address in Chapter 9).

CREATE "LIGHTHOUSES FOR CHANGE"

The beginning miles of the service quality journey can be dark and discouraging. One way to make the early going easier is to build beacons—lighthouses for change that demonstrate the effect of improved service on overall profitability, employee morale—and the employee's own bottom line. The identification of customers' service expectations and the establishment of service performance standards can be the foundation for constructing "pockets of change"—initial service quality pilot projects in specific units, departments, or branches. Success breeds success, and pilot projects that show service can be improved—and that service improvement does indeed have positive effects—can be management's most powerful weapon in converting the organization's service skeptics.

At Omega, Consultants to Bank Management, a pocket of change was the firm's Customer Service Department. The catalysts were complaints about responsiveness, shipping error rate, and the realization that for many clients, customer service *is* Omega. Omega's sales representatives were sufficiently concerned about the problem that it became customary for them to instruct clients to place product orders through the sales staff, rather than contacting the Customer Service Department directly.

"In negotiating service standards for the department, we started with a goal of 'zero errors,' then later refined that standard to two levels of errors—serious ones, like shipping the wrong product, versus making a minor typo in a shipping document that would not affect delivery," explains Controller

Ann van Oppen. "We still want people to shoot for zero errors, but we allow them to make *one* of the less serious mistakes without having it affect the reward and recognition system, which includes cash awards for error-free months."

Six months later, van Oppen says the improvement has been "spectacular," with a series of error-free months becoming the norm rather than the exception. Better yet, the company's sales force has learned to "let go." They no longer feel they need to hold onto every aspect of each transaction to make sure things are done correctly.

"The customer service representatives always felt that they were doing a good job, but now they really feel they're doing something for the company," she says. "They're working as a team, and I don't think that had been the case for a while. As a result, they are more interested in coming up with ideas that will improve procedures. After all, they have the best awareness of what their own jobs entail, and what might be done to improve policies and procedures. It all stems from increased accountability and responsibility—and from the fact that management is giving them so much support."

As a blueprint for building a lighthouse for change, the Omega experiment offers several valuable lessons. First, the company started with a highly visible area where specific problems had been identified, where standard-setting was a straightforward process, and where improvement was easy to track. Management support continues to be strong, and both service improvements and the resulting rewards have been widely publicized throughout the company. In fact, the incentive system itself has contributed to a "bandwagon" effect. Employees in other departments see the answer to that critical question, "What's in it for me?"

MANAGEMENT'S ROLE IN GETTING STARTED

Even with one or more beacons illuminating the way, organizations embarking on the service quality journey can expect problems, including service skeptics still lurking in the woods.

In identifying roadblocks to service quality in his company, one financial institution executive listed: (1) traditional views of how things should be done; (2) drawing continually toward lower transaction costs in the service delivery area; and (3) concentrating on service delivery from the viewpoint of the business, not the customer. That sums up the major barrier to getting started—the cultural barrier that we call the "Service Wall." When asked to specify "start-up problems" on the road to service quality, many of the executives we surveyed commented about colliding with the cultural status quo. The problems they listed include:

- Habit. We've always done it this way.
- Our operations mentality has been built up for decades. We're not going to change things overnight.
- Our branches are designed for efficiency and flow, not for paying attention to customers.
- Time pressures. Our branch managers feel they have other priorities.
- People don't understand what service quality is or what's in it for them. They don't know what needs to be changed.
- Disbelief. People feel that it's just another fad that will pass, and that they can wait it out. In fact, one banker joked, "I tell them, 'It's 1988. The color is mauve and the theme is Service Quality.' "

This is where senior leadership comes in—the commitment of top management to service quality and the ability to communicate that commitment. The message: "Yes, the year is 1988, but Service Quality is more than this year's theme. It is the focus for this organization, the way we are going to do business today . . . and tomorrow." Yet, in spite of all the "start-up" communication—the "kickoff" parties, the videos, the meetings—the skepticism is likely to remain.

Skepticism is built into the Service Wall, and research is one of the tools for breaking the wall down. Even service skeptics are likely to take notice when objective evidence replaces assumptions, when fact supercedes rhetoric. Obtaining that evidence requires the use of multiple research approaches directed to customers, noncustomers, and employees. Setting service performance standards based on customer expectations is also critical as a way of defining service quality for employees and providing benchmarks against which performance can be evaluated. Starting small—with organizational "pockets of change"—can help make service quality improvement seem more manageable and less elusive. One consultant compared improving service quality with losing weight; it's easiest when broken down into small achievable increments. "Losing 25 pounds may sound impossible," she said. "Losing 18 ounces a day doesn't."

NOTES

1. Berry, Leonard L. "Multiple Measures Reflect True Service Quality." *American Banker,* March 10, 1988.
2. Parasuraman, A., Zeithaml, Valarie, and Berry, Leonard L. *SERVQUAL: A Multiple-Item Scale for Measuring Customer Perceptions of Service Quality*, Cambridge, Mass.: Marketing Science Institute, 1986.
3. Berry, Leonard L. "Multiple Measures Reflect True Service Quality." *American Banker,* March 10, 1988.
4. Ibid.
5. Berry, Leonard L. "Three Approaches to Measuring Quality of Service." *American Banker,* July 9, 1986.
6. Berry, Leonard L. "Multiple Measures Reflect True Service Quality." *American Banker,* March 10, 1988.
7. Ibid.

CHAPTER 7

MARSHALLING RESOURCES
FOR SERVICE PERFORMANCE

Even if a customer only calls you once a year, he or she is going to size up your entire bank on that one telephone call. Do you have your best people on the phone, or do you put your least personable people back there because you thought they weren't good with customers? You've got it reversed if you did.

—*Richard Davis, Senior Vice President and*
Manager of Customer Service Administration,
Security Pacific National Bank

Firms noted for service excellence did not achieve that status by accident. "They make outlandish efforts to hire only the right people, to train and motivate them, and to give them the authority necessary to serve customers well. They invest earlier and much more heavily than their competitors in technology to support customer service. They keep an especially sharp eye on the competition. And they constantly ask customers to rate the quality of service they have received."[1]

Service quality research provides the basis for setting the service agenda—for pinpointing priorities and jettisoning what gets in the way. Knowing what needs to be done, however, is not the only or even the most formidable challenge. Still ahead is the challenge of effecting real change in the organization, of transforming plans into actions.

The service quality journey involves taking a close look at all of the institution's resources in light of customer expectations and service roadblocks and then taking formal steps to marshall those resources to remove the roadblocks and meet the expectations. Key steps include identifying service quality "drivers," organizing and staffing for quality, empowering service providers, and supporting service with technology, all of which are the subjects of this chapter.

THE SERVICE DRIVER

It is said so often, it now sounds trite. Nevertheless, we say it again because it is so important: *Service excellence requires the inspired leadership of top management.* Being visible, forceful, and relentless on behalf of service excellence is not something a CEO or president can delegate. Organizations that break down the "Service Wall" do so because top management makes it clear that quality is the "name of the game" and people who can't buy into that will need to work for another organization. That service quality leadership cannot be delegated is a point much in evidence in Chapter 4, the story not only of Crate & Barrel, Southwest Airlines, Randall's Food and Drug, and Washington's Park Hyatt Hotel, but also of Gordon Segal, Herbert Kelleher, Robert Onstead, and Paul Limbert.

The service leadership role of top management involves demonstrating, communicating, and reinforcing the organization-wide commitment to service quality. Articulating the vision and then underlining it through personal example are roles that top management must perform. Having said this, the building of a service culture is often boosted by the presence of a "service driver" (or several service drivers) who can take charge of the nuts and bolts of the change process and coordinate the many activities necessary to move the organization forward. Effecting cultural change can be a full-time job—particularly in a large organization—and senior management can benefit from the assistance of a service driver.

The service driver's role is to assist top management in building a service-minded culture by coordinating the introduction and implementation of new systems, processes, and programs; by identifying and supporting cultural change agents throughout the organization; by fostering inter-organizational communication and teamwork; by sharing expertise and solving problems; by helping carry top management's message to the troops; and, just as importantly, by carrying the troops' message to top management.

Just as the driver supports top management, so must top management support the driver. The whole concept crumbles if management lets the driver sink or swim on his or her own.

One bank executive surveyed cautions against the situation he sees in his own institution, where an Executive Vice President with many years of line experience was "promoted" to Director of Quality Service. "There is no system. There is no tracking. There is no slogan or series of internal programs. There is no communication other than the normal bank newspaper and video magazine. In short, like so many banks, it is lip-service programming, little else," he says.

"Thus, the employees do not view it as something to be overly concerned about. No one is worked up; no one is let go."

The role of a service driver requires a leader who can seek out other potential service leaders in the organization and draft them as sponsors of change. It calls for an awareness that leadership is by no means confined to the executive suite, that leaders can be found at any level of management and used to spread their influence horizontally and vertically by creating pockets of change whose success spurs other parts of the organization to action.

Selecting the "right" service driver is clearly critical. Indeed, the selection decision itself is symbolic of top management's true commitment to service excellence. To the degree that management selects a strong person for the job, management signals to others in the organization that the job is important. Ideally, the service driver will be someone from the upper reaches of management who has broad experience (including line experience) and who has a keen understanding of "how things get done" in the organization. The driver should also be someone who is highly credible in the organization, who can work well in an interdisciplinary arena, who can "pull" change, not just "push" change, and who has the attributes of a good salesperson—assertiveness *and* empathy. Last, but not least, the driver should be that rare person who not only has the vision and entrepreneurial instincts of a leader, but also the organizational skills of an administrator. A rare person? Yes. Impossible to find? No. Most financial institutions have individuals in management positions who possess the essential attributes. The real key is top management's willingness to make the appointment.

Keith Oosthoek, Quality of Service Manager for The Royal Bank of Canada, came up through the line and has served as both a branch and area manager. As a result, he has a chain of relationships across the country that he can call on to get things done, people who, in turn, regard him as a resource. When asked to assume the service quality position, Oosthoek agreed on one condition—that the word "programs" be dropped from the job title. "If we were to look at improving our quality of service seriously, we should not be thinking in terms of 'quick-fix' solutions," states Oosthoek.

Part of Oosthoek's job is improving the level of communication among managers, a goal at the top of his agenda at the time we interviewed him. "First, I'm getting together with 15 managers to ask them what they expect from the six major resource groups within the district from a service standpoint. What do they need to provide good service to their clients?" he said. "The next day, I'm going to sit down with the six major resource groups to find out what they can deliver. On the third day, I am going to pull the two together and have them negotiate an acceptable level of service. The managers need to understand some of the restraints, and the district people need to understand what it takes to offer a commitment to our clients."

Richard Davis also came up through the line at Security Pacific National Bank—and, in fact, still manages 3 branches, in addition to being in charge of a 25-member Quality Assurance staff serving 600 branches. His role includes frequent travel among the branches, representing senior management's commitment to service quality and answering questions or solving problems in the field "People perceive me in a dual role," he says. "Both as one of them, because just a few years ago I was managing one of our biggest offices, and as the bank's service quality expert."

At Perpetual Savings Bank in Alexandria, Virginia, the service driver role is performed by Gail George, Vice President of Training and Development. She assumed the mantle of service leadership by recognizing a problem and taking the initiative to do something about it. "In our strategic planning process, senior management sets both financial and non-financial goals, then it is up to various divisions and departments to develop strategies around those goals," she explains.

"I found that there were a number of quality initiatives in progress, but only one that was very thorough—one that existed in our branch system. The principal difficulty was that the ability to deliver high quality service often depended on people who weren't in the functional area—data processing, for example. So I suggested to our Executive Vice President that we take a look at service quality from a corporate-wide point of view. Our individual efforts were running into obstacles—maybe even setting up competing strategies—even though the goals were often the same."

George's first step was getting the stakeholders on board right away. "It's easy to write down service quality as a corporate goal, more difficult to make people understand what's in it for them," she says. "We're doing it from the top down, with senior management meetings followed by one-on-one meetings. It's important to make people understand they are very much part of the ownership."

ORGANIZING FOR SERVICE QUALITY

The process of institutionalizing service quality does not stop with the appointment of a service driver. The next step is to organize a service quality group that reflects a cross section of the organization's functions. The service driver typically would head this group. If properly executed, the group will help spread "ownership" for service quality throughout the organization and provide an infrastructure for taking action, without saddling the culture change effort with red tape and political maneuvering. Members of this group should retain their respective positions so that they continue to experience directly the realities of the service system and communicate with others in the organization from a base of maximum credibility. One consultant we interviewed described the purpose of a service quality group in the following way:

> Basically, the responsibility of a service quality task force is to look at the issue of improved service in terms of what is best for the organization as a whole. The task force acts as a clearinghouse for ideas, a reporting mechanism for senior management, and a study group for evaluating the effects of individual quality improvement efforts and making additional recommendations.
>
> Pulling a cross section of people from a variety of areas improves the chances of covering all the important issues that surface. That's true even if you start small, with a focus on one particular area for improvement. For example, reducing the length of teller lines in the branches may mean reevaluating tellers' job descriptions, streamlining behind-the-counter procedures, and changing computer systems. Right away, you are involving personnel, operations, and audit people, as well as branch personnel. When you look at any given policy, how that policy is set, and all the different parts of the organization that are affected by a policy revision, you begin to see the ramifications of change.

What to call the service quality group (or groups) is important, especially since these groups usually are established early in the culture change process when credibility needs to be bolstered. The consultant we just quoted uses the term "task force," as do a number of financial institutions. To us, "task force" means "temporary," an ill-fitting meaning. Unless the intention of management is to dismantle a group once it completes a specific task or series of tasks, we recommend a different term, for example, "board," "committee," or "group."

Three Examples

At Perpetual Savings Bank, members of the Service Quality Steering Group include representatives from each major functional area—both line and staff areas—and others from areas such as corporate planning. According to Gail George, the Group's charter consists of six major responsibilities:

1. Provide leadership to the individual divisions represented.
2. Identify opportunities for service quality improvement and request action for improvement.
3. Coordinate cross-functional initiatives.
4. Receive reports and review progress on the service quality initiatives of individual units. "That includes reviewing results of actions individual managers are taking, reinforcing their efforts, and borrowing ideas from other areas."
5. Provide individual and unit recognition and reward for achievement of service quality initiatives—primarily identifying service "heroes" and making sure that successes are broadcast through the organization.
6. Track gains made through service quality improvement efforts, and report those gains "up, down, and across" the organization.

"While there was belief that nothing would happen without top-down involvement, there was little consensus about who should be in the Service Quality Steering Group," George says. "The ideal seemed to be a diagonal slice of the corporation, to include people who are close to the customer. Consequently, each function head decides who needs to be in the Group from his or her area, and each department sets up its own mechanism for gathering information for the Group. Some areas have their own internal steering committees made up of employees at all levels with vice presidents serving on the corporate steering committee."

George adds that, initially, the main concern of the Service Quality Steering Group was communication—how to get employees excited about the opportunities improved service quality offers. To that end, three primary objectives were established:

1. Developing a leadership style that is conducive to service. "We know that leadership is basic to companies that have been successful in improving quality of ser-

vice. We need people who lead from whatever spot they may be standing in, who look at improving Service Quality as *their* jobs—not that of senior management."

2. Developing cross functional work processes with an emphasis on the internal supplier chain and its impact on the external customer. "We need a much more collaborative style to eliminate internal conflicts or competition that may affect external service delivery," George explains.

3. Establishing measurement systems to provide ongoing feedback. "Each function needs to have a measurement component tied directly to meeting customers' expectations both internal and external to tell us if we are getting better over time."

Bank of Boston's Massachusetts Banking Division has both a Customer Service Assurance Department and a service quality task force. The Customer Service Assurance Department reports to the Director of Human Resources and Customer Service, who reports, in turn, to the Division Executive of Massachusetts Banking. The objectives of Customer Service Assurance are:

1. Provide direction for achieving customer service leadership.

2. Inculcate dedication to service through programs, compensation, and recognition systems, training, measurement, feedback, policies, and procedures.

3. Demonstrate superior customer service in the handling of complaints.

4. Interface with senior management and professionals to assure quality of customer service.

The service quality task force is chaired by the Director of Human Resources and Customer Service, and consists of the directors of major line and support functions. Department Executive D. Bruce Wheeler articulates its objective as developing . . . "strategic objectives and appropriate tactics in support of our goal to be leaders in customer service."

As an example of a service improvement success, Wheeler cites the management of a major acquisition which was placed with the Customer Service Assurance function. "The primary objective of the acquisition project was 100 percent retention of balances. It was felt that customer service was the way to achieve this objective. The bottom line is that 1 month after the acquisition, the balances attributable to acquired customers had increased by over $2 million."

National Westminster Bank USA started its quality improvement effort in 1985 with the formation of an executive steering committee to set policy and lead the overall change process. Next a quality council made up of managers from each part of the bank was established to coordinate interdivisional projects and to further facilitate the improvement process bank-wide.

Quality improvement teams composed of managers at all levels were formed in each division, with the responsibility of finding service improvement opportunities and developing "quality action teams" to analyze the details and implement the required changes. By 1987, more than 100 quality action teams were in place, finding ways to reduce mail room missorts, reduce or eliminate errors of all types on applications completed in the branch system, and improve the timeliness of service delivery. NatWest also established a quality improvement division to provide training services and, in general, help keep the quality process moving.[2]

Neil Metviner, Vice President and Department Head of Quality Improvement, comments, "The organizational structure has allowed the company to effect the change required by having the entire company take part. We have been able to bring about the changes needed and foster a team approach to quality improvement."

In considering the Perpetual, Bank of Boston, and NatWest organizational approaches together, the similarities are more striking than the differences. All three banks are taking a proactive, aggressive posture to service quality improvement. The mandates to the organizational groups created are to search out opportunities for improving the service system. The organizational mechanisms put into place are ongoing rather than temporary and provide for both high level interorganizational participation and "grassroots" involvement in the various divisions and operating units. In each case, the banks have organized to coordinate the overall quality initiative, to continually dispense and receive information to keep the process moving, and to encourage subunits in the institution to take action—to care about service quality and to do something about it.

The Perpetual, Bank of Boston, and NatWest examples also demonstrate variation. A fundamental organizational decision concerns whether or not to form a service quality "department." Among other functions, this department might implement service quality research, training, and communications programs or work closely with other departments on these matters. In addition, the customer complaint management program could be housed in this unit.

The advantages of centralizing some or all of these functions in a service quality department can be significant. For one thing, a service quality staff assures full-time attention to quality management and implementation issues. Also, the creation of a service quality staff could result in the assembling of a core of expertise in specialized areas such as service quality research and training that wouldn't otherwise exist.

With the potential advantages of a service quality department come these caveats. First, the department should be kept as small as possible. It is critical to avoid the mistake of trying to solve one bureaucracy's problems by creating another bureaucracy. Second, every possible means should be used to avoid the impression in the organization that service quality is the responsibility of the service quality department; the department should be positioned as a resource for the rest of the organization, and the theme "quality is everyone's job" should be sounded at every opportunity.

STAFFING FOR QUALITY

Selecting the right individual to help "drive" the service improvement process and institutionalizing the process from an organizational standpoint are critical steps. Also critical is staffing the service system with people having the capacity to serve effectively.

It stands to reason that service can only be as good as the

people who provide it. In many financial institutions, mediocre service quality reflects the fact that service providers are frequently poorly paid and poorly managed, replaceable cogs in a wheel that goes nowhere. In other institutions, an operations-oriented approach to the business has put the emphasis on technical abilities at the expense of skills and traits necessary to support a service culture.

When asked to identify the major roadblocks to service quality in his institution, one banker stated, "We have required branch employees to be operationally proficient, but have not selected customer contact staff on their interpersonal skills, warm and outgoing personalities, or ability to resolve conflict. In addition, our interbranch rotation transfer program has denied management trainees and more experienced platform personnel the opportunity to identify with their customers and their market area. The result is a lack of understanding and empathy."

In some cases, the basis of the problem is who does the hiring. It is not uncommon in financial institutions for the personnel office—located at corporate headquarters—to interview and hire all personnel. Operating unit managers may not even meet new hires until the first day on the job! In the book *Bankers Who Sell,* Berry, Futrell, and Bowers discuss bank managers who complain bitterly about the "warm bodies" the personnel department sends them and about the unfairness of a system in which they are accountable for the performance of their units, but have little or no control over who gets hired.[3]

A bank executive surveyed for the present book adds, "Recruiting procedures are often a roadblock when those responsible for the human resources of an organization are not sufficiently oriented to the need for recruiting people who either already have a strong service orientation or who can be trained to develop such an orientation."

We believe many institutions could take a big step forward in the service quality journey by rethinking traditional personnel recruiting assumptions and practices. The key to improved staffing is to start with the customer and work backwards from there. The theme of this book is that service excellence starts with understanding customer expectations for the service, and there is no reason to depart from this theme when considering the staffing function. Simply put, what financial institutions need to do is to identify customer expectations and establish service standards based on those expectations (as we have already discussed) and then make sure that hiring criteria, hiring methods, and compensation packages are sufficient to attract new hires that can meet the standards.

When institutions do not set service standards at all, or when they do set service standards but do not use them to establish hiring criteria, then it is simply "potluck" in terms of building capacity to meet customer expectations.

Financial institution executives need to start thinking of jobs as "internal products," employees as "internal customers," and employee recruiting as a marketing issue. They need to think like marketers when competing for talent to increase the probabilities of attracting talent. They need to use nontraditional media to attract job candidates, for example, recruiting parties, job fairs, employee-get-an-employee campaigns. They need to be more thorough in evaluating candidates. They need to be willing to challenge old assumptions such as the common assumption that college graduates are too educated or too expensive for certain types of service positions. They need to make sure that operating unit managers have the final say in who gets hired and, more generally, that line managers and personnel specialists work together closely to define hiring criteria. Most of all, they need to remember that to the customer, the service provider *is* the service and it makes no sense to spend vast sums of money on service facilities and then insist on bargains in staffing these facilities.

Tom Peters writes, "The task of transforming raw recruits into committed stars, able to cope with the pace of change that is becoming normal, begins with the recruiting process per se. The best follow three tenets, unfortunately ignored by most: (1) spend time, and lots of it; (2) insist that line people dominate the process; and (3) don't waffle about the qualities you are looking for in candidates."[4]

Concerning the latter point, what qualities should be considered? What constitutes a "service orientation"? The ability to make decisions and solve problems is high on the list. So is sensitivity—a concern for others. Flexibility is also important, as are good oral communication skills, dependability, judgment, and the ability to work as part of a team.[5] An extremely important characteristic is enthusiasm. Stanley J. Calderon, President and CEO of Bank One, Lafayette, says, "We are trying to inject another facet into the quality of our bank; that is, the application of enthusiasm to the delivery of customer service. We believe this may be a secret ingredient in the delivery of service quality—not just to wait on customers courteously and expeditiously, but to do it with enthusiasm."

EMPOWERING FOR QUALITY

Even if the staffing function is handled well, the potential for service excellence will be limited to the extent that committed and qualified service providers are unnecessarily restricted in their freedom to serve. Unfortunately, financial institutions are among the worst offenders in shackling frontline service providers with thick policy manuals and strict sets of rules concerning the service role. The end result is more standardized service that is also more inflexible—more "by-the-book" service that is also more regimented.

The proneness to thick policy manuals in the financial services sector is understandable, an artifact of the fiduciary nature—and extensive regulation—of the business. However, this by-the-book orientation is also a consequence of managements that value efficiency over effectiveness and that are reluctant to trust the judgment of frontline service providers.

Two stories surfacing during research for this book illustrate the importance of building a culture that encourages a reasonable degree of service freedom. The first story concerns a branch manager who kept irate customers waiting outside in the freezing cold while he stood in view just inside the door, watch in hand, waiting for "opening time" to let the customers in. When asked why, the manager replied that banking law prevented him from opening early.

The second story, told by William C. Nelson, former Executive Vice President for First Republic Bank in Houston, concerns an agitated customer whose automatic teller machine (ATM) card was "eaten" by a machine just as she was getting ready to go on a trip. "She was a long way from the bank and we don't have branches. She was livid! So she called a bank officer, who offered to send the $200 she needed out to her in a cab. The customer was absolutely floored. She not only stopped complaining, but now raves on and on about our fantastic service. And her husband, who is the head of a major investment banking company, tells the story at gatherings of business people. The interesting thing is that if our banking officer had asked anyone first, the idea would have been rejected. However, it certainly was the smart thing to do in that situation."

Retelling these two stories together is instructive because they convey the flip sides of the freedom-to-serve issue—the significant potential to destroy or build an institution's service reputation that relates to service providers' perceived freedom to do what makes sense, even if that means bending certain policies. In the first story, the manager confused tradition with regulation, and hurt his bank in the eyes of customers. In the second case, the banker did the right thing for the customer and the bank, but would have been "shot down" had he first requested permission—which means that many officers in that bank would *not* have accommodated the customer had they been the ones contacted.

Clearly, one of the keys to service excellence is empowering service providers to serve—giving them the flexibility to use judgment in the service role, the training to support their judgment and hone their skills, and the sense of ownership in service excellence so that they will want to make special efforts for customers.

In making the case for empowerment, we are not advocating anarchy. We are not suggesting that operational policy be cavalierly swept away or that bankers be less careful with other people's money. What we are advocating is pushing as much authority and responsibility as possible downward in the organizational hierarchy, close to the customer. We are urging that management take a hard and continuing look at the institution's "rule book," eliminating or modifying those restrictions that are not vital, that interfere with service quality, and that spoil the creative part of service for service employees.

Not all employees will flourish in a less regimented service culture. Some employees are more comfortable when everything is spelled out for them, and financial institutions may have attracted more than their fair share of these people. Nevertheless, most financial service providers would much rather provide good service than bad and, given time to develop confidence in the changing culture, will flourish with added service freedom.

One executive comments that the overriding theme among his institution's branch managers is, "Let me manage. Let me run my branch in a way that best serves the customer. In situations where I've got a policy or procedure that needs to be bent or changed to meet the customer's needs, let me do it."

In a published interview, James Houghton, Chairman and CEO of Corning Glass Works, sounds a similar note. Asked where quality commitment has to start—top down, bottom up, or all at once—Houghton responded:[6]

> It must start at the top. There's no getting away from it. . . . Along with pressure from the top, the second key area of pressure is from the folks at the bottom of the organization. If there is commitment at the top, the people at the bottom quickly become committed themselves. They're saying, 'Where have you guys been all my life? We know how to do the job. Give us the tools and let us get on with it.'

NIGHTMARE IN SOUTH FLORIDA: THE LOTTYE CARLIN STORY

The case of Lottye Carlin versus a Florida bank is a classic—if extreme—example of what can happen to customer service when an overblown corporate bureaucracy is combined with a lack of initiative in settling a problem. As reported in *The Wall Street Journal,*[7] Mrs. Carlin's 8-year nightmare began when the bank mistakenly issued a MasterCard to a "Lothye" Carlin after Mrs. Carlin had responded to the offer of a credit card to her late husband. Lottye Carlin never received the Master-Card, but apparently someone did. Soon, the bank's collection department was calling at all hours of the day—more than 50 calls in all—to demand payment of more than $2,000 in charges.

Mrs. Carlin's response to the calls was usually the same, "Show me an itemized statement with my signature on it." The callers from the bank refused, one commenting that such a statement would cost too much to produce. Another said, "Pay the $2,000 or never get credit again."

That was no idle threat, as Mrs. Carlin found in 1981 after putting down a $9,000 deposit on a new condominium, only to have her mortgage application denied because of a bad credit rating. In an attempt to settle the matter, she drove to Miami for a meeting with a member of the bank's collection department—where she was told that clearing up the problem would cost her $50, the fee for closing the account. Her response, "I wasn't going to pay them 50 cents because I didn't owe them a nickel."

It wasn't over yet. Through a settlement with the condominium developer, she was able to retrieve only half of her down payment; the rest was forfeited because of her inability to get financing. Then 8 months after offering to settle for $50, the bank sued to collect the entire $2,064.64—only to drop the suit the morning of the trial. Mrs. Carlin then demanded that the bank pay her legal expenses and was accordingly awarded $3,500, a decision that was overturned in 1985 on the basis of a bank appeal. By then, Mrs. Carlin's 6-year battle had cost her more than $8,000.

In February 1985, Lottye Carlin turned the tables and sued the bank for malicious prosecution. The day before the trial, the bank agreed to pay $150,000 to settle the suit—and also agreed, at Mrs. Carlin's insistence, to apologize in writing. "Lottye Carlin fell into a meat grinder back in 1979 when the card was first issued, and it just kept grinding and grinding," comments David Baron, her attorney.[8]

The Lottye Carlin story is one of gross insensitivity and lack of accountability. Starting with the initial misspelling of the name on the credit card, the compounding of error upon error reaches the point of farce. It seems incredible that no one would listen, that no one would send an itemized statement upon request, that no one would admit that the bank had made a mistake. Part of the answer is probably "policies and procedures"—that everyone involved from the bank side was following the "letter of the law." But it is also evident, very simply, that no one really cared.

THINK HIGH TECH, NOT JUST HIGH TOUCH

Thus far, our emphasis in this chapter has been on the human side of service delivery. Another principal resource for service quality is technology—in part because of its potential for supporting people in the service delivery role. Technology offers one of the best opportunities for financial institutions to improve service efficiency and productivity. To think of service excellence only in terms of "personal service" is a serious error.

As H. Jim Harrold, former Vice President of Sales and Service for Canadian Imperial Bank of Commerce observes, "Technologists and systems support people are just as important as everyone else. That message is important to get across because all too frequently people think of customer service only in terms of face-to-face contact. We have to recognize that service quality happens whenever anyone deals with us in any way, whether it be through plastic, through an ATM, or through a merchant's terminal that has our name on it. That's all part of service quality."

For virtually all financial institutions, the real service quality opportunity lies in high tech *and* high touch, rather than one or the other. High technology can speed up service delivery, increase reliability, and liberate service personnel to provide more and better services. High touch capability can mean more personalized and customized service, more effective cross-selling, and more customer confidence in the technology (because the customer knows someone will help if the technology fails).[9]

The high tech/high touch institution gives its customers a

choice; the institution serves its customers situationally, depending on their preferences and specific requirements of the moment. Management sees technology and personal service as mutually supportive of each other, as interconnected thrusts for the future, rather than as competing alternatives.[10]

Technology is a means to an end, not the end in itself. What technologies are best for a given institution depend on that institution's strategy. The strategy comes first—then the decisions that help support it. For example, a client-based relationship banking strategy requires different technology than a "plain vanilla," mass market strategy—even though technology is important to each. Whereas relationship banking calls for comprehensive client information systems, integrated account statements, and technology-based "core" services (for example, financial planning systems), mass-market banking could involve electronic delivery systems, teller station automation, and automated systems for opening accounts and lending money.

At the Bank of Boston, retail customers applying for loans can phone a branch-based lender who—thanks to a direct tie-in to the credit bureau and a computer program that facilitates lending decisions—can render a decision on 70 percent of the loan requests within 30 minutes. The remaining loans requiring further analysis are generally completed within 24 hours.

"What we've done through the installation of our branch phone centers is offer much better customer service at a lower cost, and our customers are responding fantastically well," comments Department Executive-Massachusetts Banking D. Bruce Wheeler. "The phone centers free the people in the branches for selling services. It creates time in the branch."

The objectives here were improving service, lowering costs, cutting transaction time—and lending more money. The tech/touch solution meets all criteria.

The importance of technology in improving service quality can hardly be overstated. When the financial services executives we surveyed indicated how they improved service quality by streamlining procedures, centralizing given functions, improving communications, and changing the way branches or departments conduct business, technology was usually a factor.

The successful application of technology, however, is no sure thing. The wrong technology, or the right technology improperly integrated into the service system or improperly presented to its "customers," will likely represent expensive mistakes. It is the design of a service process, with the correct blend of human and inanimate functions, that meets customer expectations and minimizes waste, that helps institutions head in the right direction.

SERVICE QUALITY IS A DESIGN ISSUE

Service quality needs to be a forethought, not an afterthought. It needs to be a way of thinking that influences each step in the development of new services, technologies, and facilities. Designing quality into new offerings instead of "force-fitting" quality initiatives *after the fact* results in higher reliability for customers, higher morale for employees, and higher productivity for the organization.

Inattention to user requirements and carelessness with details are, unfortunately, all too common in the design of service offerings. A service is a process, and the key is to design quality into the process. This is the philosophy of W. Edwards Deming, the famed statistician who helped Japanese industry improve product quality. Deming believes that fully 85 percent of all quality problems are a function of poor process design or other sources not controlled by the worker. Although his estimate may be too high for service businesses, his point is valid— quality needs to be built into the process.

At this stage in the book, it is apparent that there are no simple answers or formulas for service excellence. Service excellence comes from a "chemistry" of leadership, solid information, organizational infrastructure, good people who are free to serve, technology that supports their efforts—and other ingredients yet to be discussed. Service excellence is "heart" not just "things," execution not just strategy, little ideas not just big ideas. It is the marshalling of resources—human and otherwise—in a well-designed service system.

We close the chapter with a small story that illustrates the chemistry of service quality. The story comes from a banker in our survey who told how a manager in his company had turned around a department that was unprofitable and noted for poor morale. "In implementing some quality management techniques, the head of the department worked very closely with his staff, and to a large extent gave them the authority to make the changes they needed to make—nothing dramatic, changes the manager calls 'small winds.' For example, he reorganized the work locations. He put in a telephone where records were, so that when people had to look things up, they didn't have to hang up the phone and come back to make another call. And he put a buzzer on the telephone to alert the staff that a customer had been left on hold. Little things like that."

Little things that work. As a result of these little things, the banker adds, the department has become very profitable, productivity has improved, and morale has gone "through the roof." Staff turnover dropped by 30 percent. "To the department head, it was just common sense—something you just do. To him, that's part of how you serve the customer."

NOTES

1. Uttal, Bro. "Companies that Serve You Best." *Fortune,* December 7, 1987, p. 99.
2. Deutsch, Howard and Metviner, Neil J. "Quality in Banking: The Competitive Edge." *Bank Administration,* April 1987.
3. Berry, Leonard L, Futrell, Charles M., and Bowers, Michael R. *Bankers Who Sell: Improving Selling Effectiveness in Banking.* Chicago: Bank Marketing Association, and Homewood, IL: Dow Jones-Irwin, 1985, pp. 58–59.
4. Peters, Tom. *Thriving on Chaos.* New York: Alfred A. Knopf, 1987, p. 315.
5. DeSatnick, Robert L. "Building the Customer-Oriented Work Force." *Training and Development Journal,* March 1987.
6. "The Chairman Doesn't Blink." *Quality Progress,* March 1987, p. 22.
7. De Cordoba, Jose. "Beating the Bank: How One Woman Fought a Credit-Card Error—and Won." *The Wall Street Journal,* July 9, 1987, p. 31.

8. Ibid.
9. Berry, Leonard L. "Big Ideas in Services Marketing." *The Journal of Consumer Marketing,* Spring 1986.
10. Berry, Leonard L. and Reider, George A. "Bankers Should Reflect on Importance and Use of Technology." *American Banker,* July 9, 1986.

CHAPTER 8

PREPARING PEOPLE TO
SERVE BETTER

Quality is our only form of patent protection.
*—James D. Robinson, CEO, American Express
Company, as quoted in* Business Week[1]

People must be willing to serve, as well as able to serve. A critical step toward service excellence is investing in the skill and knowledge development of servers, giving them the preparation to serve and in so doing, stoking their desire to serve.

The term "training"—as conventional and familiar as it is—is too limiting for the service quality journey. One banker we surveyed comments that "training only gets at the skills. We want people to have knowledge." Adds retailer Stanley Marcus,[2] "You can train dogs and bears, but you educate people. That's because people have to understand *why* they should do something. It's true for customers. And it's true for all your employees."

Understanding *why* is the key phrase. Not just *what* needs to be done or *how* services should be performed, but *why* service excellence is important to both the organization and the individual employee. An educational system that truly develops people by combining skill and knowledge improvement and tying it to the overall goals of the organization can help instill both the willingness and the ability to serve. This is why one banker extols the value of "a grassroots program to acquaint all employees with the meaning of quality—what does it mean to each of us, and just as important, what can each of us do to make a difference?"

Developing the skills and knowledge of employees to support an internal service culture is much like the service quality journey itself. Both are never ending. Just as the improvement of service quality should not be regarded as a "program," neither should training and education be treated as an "event"—a class or workshop that fills 3 days or a week, then is gone.

As C. J. Lendrum, Deputy Director, U.K. Retail Services for Barclays Bank, London observes, "Reinforcing the message constantly is very important. If one just has a series of two-day training courses in a hotel somewhere, then sends employees back to their branches, the quality improvement effort will fall apart. It needs constant attention."

Instead, skill and knowledge development is a journey in itself—an unending road with many stops to refresh learned skills that may have grown stale; renew motivation; upgrade knowledge about customers, products, the organization, and the competition; and teach new skills that reflect changing customer expectations, strategies, and technologies. Skill and knowledge development is a complex and many-faceted activity that must be planned, supported, and measured as carefully as service quality improvement itself, and conducted with an eye toward the same bottom line—meeting customer expectations.

THE ROLE OF SKILL AND KNOWLEDGE DEVELOPMENT IN SHAPING ORGANIZATIONAL VALUES

Cultural change requires open, active, and constant communication. The power of training and education as a primary channel of communication in supporting cultural change should not be underestimated. In addition to teaching job-critical skills and helping people grow professionally, employee training and education can pave the way for change by opening minds and clearing out false assumptions. It can stimulate people and keep them excited about their work, and about their new challenges. *It can ignite enthusiasm.*

Thomas C. Vick, Senior Vice President at First American Corporation in Nashville, tells the story of a call his operations "hot desk" received from an outlying bank, requesting directions to a local hospital for a customer who was scheduled for surgery. The person at the desk not only provided directions, but also offered his home phone number in case the customer got lost. Sure enough, the customer called back on Saturday morning for further directions. The banker then volunteered to meet the customer and drive him to the hospital personally. "And you can believe we have that customer's loyalty for life," Vick adds.

We tell this story because of what it illustrates about enthusiasm—and service. True service involves taking advantage of opportunities, showing initiative and taking responsibility, not only meeting—but also exceeding—customer expectations. The seeds of true service are such values as caring and helping, values that need to be ingrained in the culture of the organization, values that become reflexive. For this to happen, these values should be woven into every training or education program offered, every meeting held. No role for skill and knowledge development is more important than the building and nurturing of an organizational value system.

Skill and Knowledge Development Cannot Stand Alone

A "quality service" culture means just that—quality service is a primary focus, and as such permeates every aspect and activity of the organization. Skill and knowledge development is a primary—but not the only—means of value development. Training and education initiatives will yield more powerful results to the extent that other value-shaping actions both precede and reinforce them. These actions include:

- A clearly stated corporate mission that establishes service excellence as a key strategic priority.
- The articulation of values—both those already a part of the culture and those new ones the institution wishes to establish.
- Service role definitions that are consistent with customer expectations.

- Specific performance standards for each service role based on customer expectations.
- Individual performance objectives, based on the overall service standards, and reflective of the capabilities, experience, and customer base of the service provider.
- Individual performance measurement and appraisal linked to service standards and objectives.
- Rewards and recognitions linked to objective measurements of service performance.

Training and education can nurture service-minded values, and service-minded values can give new meaning to training and education. Skill and knowledge development cannot stand alone. Indeed, if the elements enumerated above are missing, skill and knowledge development will simply be a waste of money.

IS IT A SKILL AND KNOWLEDGE DEVELOPMENT PROBLEM?

One of the classic misconceptions about skill and knowledge development is that it is the key to all performance and attitude problems. In working with financial institutions over the years, we continue to be amazed at the number of problems defined as "needing training," when in fact the problem is rooted in service roles that need to be simplified, conflicting objectives that need to be reconciled, or something else. We advise that management conduct a needs assessment before reaching for the training and education "pill" as a cure for organizational ills. Answers to the following questions, based on work by Mager and Pipe,[3] will be helpful in determining if skill and knowledge development is the appropriate solution to an existing problem.

1. *What is the performance discrepancy?* What is the difference between what is being done and what is supposed to be done?

2. *Is the discrepancy important?* Why? What would happen if let alone?

3. *Is it a skill deficiency?* Could the employee do it if his or her life depended on it?

4. *Could the employee do it in the past?* Has the employee either forgotten the skills or that the performance is still expected?

5. *Is the skill used often?* How often? Does the employee receive feedback on performance?

6. *Is there a simpler way to do the job?* Would redesigning the job solve the problem?

7. *Does the employee have what it takes?* Does the employee have the capabilities? Is the employee overqualified?

8. *Is the desired performance punishing for the employee?* What is the consequence of performing as desired? Is the expected task punishing in some way?

9. *Is nonperformance rewarding?* What is the result of doing the job the employee's way? Is nonperformance rewarded in some way—with extra attention, perhaps?

10. *Does performance really matter?* What is the consequence of performing? Of not performing?

11. *Are there obstacles to performing?* Does the employee know what is expected? Does the employee lack authority, time, or tools? Is the employee restricted by policies, procedures, or other job demands?

12. *Which solution is best?* Are some solutions impossible or inappropriate to implement? What are the costs involved? Which solutions offer the best return on investment? What are we best equipped to try?

Just as building a service culture starts with research to better understand customer expectations and how well they are being met, so designing skill and knowledge development programs begins with research to determine what employees really need to perform excellently. As Mager and Pipe write,[4] "Until the problem is understood in greater detail, proposing a solution is simply shooting from the hip."

WHAT DO PEOPLE NEED TO KNOW?

Equipping financial institution employees with the proper mix of skills and knowledge has become a rather tall order. First of all, employees need job-critical technical skills to fulfill their roles of commercial lender, teller, proof operator, customer service representative, auditor, systems technician, branch manager, and so on. In a developing service culture, some of those basic skills may change as job descriptions shift to reflect the service emphasis.

Often, specific skill training in appropriate aspects of providing service to internal or external customers will also be needed: how to answer the telephone, how to handle irate customers, how to communicate, how to coach service providers. And since "service culture" includes "sales culture," customer contact personnel require sales skill training. On top of it all, making the service quality journey requires knowledge—understanding the "why" and the "what" in addition to knowing the "how."

Training and education for service quality improvement is an exercise in closing gaps. In particular, skill and knowledge development can help close Gap 3, the difference between service specifications and the level of service actually delivered. As we discussed earlier, Gap 3 occurs when employees lack the willingness and/or the ability to perform the service. Carefully designed skill and knowledge development initiatives support not only the ability to serve, but, less obviously, the willingness to serve. This is so because motivation is partly a function of preparedness. People who feel unprepared to perform a service are unlikely to be highly motivated to perform it. In effect, well-executed skill and knowledge development breeds confidence, and confidence is a motivator!

What Senior Executives Need

The essential role of senior management in service quality training and education, as it is in all activities related to service quality, is to provide overall direction and support. In the words of Timothy Creedon, former Executive Vice President for Valley National Bank in Phoenix, "Senior executives must create the enthusiasm. Enthusiasm is like rain. If it does not start at the top, you will never find it at the bottom."

To help create that enthusiasm, senior executives should be first in line for service quality training and education. And a key focus of these developmental activities should be understanding the customer, which is integral to all future decisions concerning service quality improvement. Senior executive programming should include the results of customer expectations and perceptions research, which can be used to build awareness, commitment, and consensus on direction. Senior executives also need to understand the strategic, bottom-line importance of quality, what is getting in the way of quality in the organization, and their roles in overcoming these obstacles and leading cultural change.

The service leadership role—and how to take it forward —is the most likely emphasis for skill and knowledge building early in the process. "After the initial discussion of the importance of service quality, the customer research results, and service gaps, senior executives were excited, enthused and perplexed," says a consultant who is guiding an Eastern bank through a service quality improvement effort. "They needed help identifying what the next steps should be and how to deal with individual issues raised, particularly how to operationalize the commitment they'd gotten from top management."

Issues of particular interest included:

- Setting performance standards that were definitive enough to act upon and be measured.
- Encouraging interdivisional team building.
- Defining the powers of interdivisional teams—defining their roles as decision-making bodies.
- Acting on the concept of "quality as a design issue" —reflecting quality in every activity, from systems and service design to planning marketing programs.
- Identifying and solving problems.
- Establishing reward and recognition initiatives.
- Developing interpersonal communication skills.
- Building a communication system that includes feedback mechanisms.

All are important issues, and all provide the opportunity for ongoing skill and knowledge development activities aimed at senior executives. But as the consultant we interviewed comments, "Senior executives are more difficult to assemble for knowledge-building sessions that other groups, and are less likely to require uniform, across-the-board subject matter." Accordingly, it is easy to fall prey to the temptation of treating skill and knowledge development for senior executives as an event rather than as a process, of mounting a 2-day service quality program for these executives and then assuming they are "trained." Well-conceived skill and knowledge development programming builds commitment, awareness, competence— and confidence—and it is just as important that it be ongoing for senior executives as for any other group.

What Middle Managers Need

"Middle managers are the key," says Timothy Creedon. "They need quality service training *before* the line service provider. If they do not accept that quality service is a 'product' with economic value, there will be no change in the level of service in that unit."

Creedon is not alone in recognizing the importance of middle managers in service improvement efforts. For these efforts to yield results, financial institutions must strive to develop service leadership skills in the managers and supervisors for whom frontline service providers work. Leadership skills development at this level of management is essential.

Willis Rhodes, Executive Vice President of Operations and Information Systems, First American Bank in Nashville, states, "You'd be amazed at the number of industries, especially banking, with supervisors who have never learned how to do a job description, recruit, or manage and motivate people. They need to know what makes people tick."

Gary McCuen, Vice President and Manager of Corporate Service Quality for Bank of America, adds, "This organization has a huge population of customer service people who are on the phone all day, and they need some very specific kinds of training. The same thing is true of tellers. In talking with management groups, what we try to do is get them to take ownership of the process, lead it—and understand that *they* have to do it. If they don't do it, neither will the rest of their people."

Middle managers need to be the on-the-spot service leaders who accept responsibility for taking senior management's mandate and direction for service quality and translating it into the day-to-day reality of service delivery. Only middle managers can play this role since virtually everyone in the organization reports to them. Middle managers need to learn how to:

- Select people with excellent service potential.
- Set and revise job objectives.
- Build teams.
- Solve problems.
- Evaluate progress against objectives.

Middle managers need to develop communication skills that will help them lead and motivate the members of their teams; they need to learn to question, listen, empathize, praise, and offer constructive feedback. Communication skills are especially critical for two of the roles middle managers must play—team leader and individual coach.

As team leaders, middle managers should be conducting group meetings to identify and solve service problems, develop service skills and knowledge, celebrate achievement, and create and sustain a sense of teamwork.

As coaches, they should be helping individual team members develop and improve the skills needed to meet customer expectations, including handling the rich variety of customer questions, special requirements, and problems that surface every day.

Sales research performed by Omega for the Consumer Bankers Association showed that branch managers who can also function as sales managers are the key to strong-selling branches. Skills exhibited by these branch managers include the ability to weld their branch staffs into sales teams, plan and run effective sales meetings, coach and provide feedback to sellers, work with sellers to set sales objectives, conduct performance planning and evaluation sessions, and identify and remove obstacles to selling.[5] Skill in communicating pervades this list of attributes.

As we suggested earlier in the book, leadership is the cornerstone of service excellence, and communication is the cornerstone of leadership. Middle managers have a crucial service leadership role to play and need to learn how to play it. Communication skill training should be a central focus.

What Frontline Service Providers Need

Tellers, commercial lenders, platform officers, customer service representatives, receptionists—these are the people in the trenches who must be skillful and knowledgeable in the daily quest for service excellence. Once again, communication skills are center stage.

Excellent communication skills relate directly to the service performance dimensions of assurance, responsiveness, and empathy. Key skills include:

- Active listening.
- Open-ended questioning to determine customer needs and problems.
- Dealing with unrealistic customer expectations and defusing customer anger.
- Telephone etiquette.
- Problem solving.
- Nonverbal communications—from eye contact to service-oriented posture.

A customer's reaction to most service encounters will be based in part on the standard of communication involved. Was the employee friendly and courteous? Was the employee clear and easy to understand? Did the employee appear interested in serving? Did the employee use the customer's name? Did the employee give the customer his or her undivided attention? Did the employee thank the customer?

How a financial institution communicates with its customers is a reflection of how it values them. Making a commitment to improve the communication skills of service providers is one of the most important things an institution can do to strengthen its quality of service reputation.[6]

Sharing center stage with communication skills is service knowledge—knowledge of the true meaning of service and its importance, knowledge of customer expectations, knowledge of the work role—its scope, dimensions and priorities, knowledge of institution policies and procedures, their rationale, and how to get around the ones that have no rationale and that needlessly frustrate customers, and knowledge of products.

One of the toughest educational challenges that financial institutions face is equipping service providers with a solid understanding of the features and benefits of numerous services. Some services will be quite similar to others in the line, some quite complex, some subject to constant interest rate shifts. Moreover, the service lineup keeps changing as new services are added. Yet, the challenge must be met because knowing which services are exactly right for a particular customer is a key to service excellence.

United Bank of Denver addresses the challenge by combining a "Product of the Month" program with a semiannual program in which all new employees spend 2 weeks familiarizing themselves with the service departments they rely on in their jobs, and with all the products the bank offers. "We're very committed to product training, because if people don't understand the products, they can't sell them. It's very apparent. We can see it in the sales records," says Executive Vice President Beverly Haddon.

"One example is IRAs, which weren't being sold because they were too complicated. Asset management products fall into another group that we're trying to sell more aggressively. For a while, we addressed the problem by producing brochures and holding general meetings for our bankers, but these services still weren't being sold. So, I sat down and talked with them and found out the bankers simply couldn't answer the questions they were asked. The solution was a half-day seminar that involved role-playing and covered product features in-depth. Suddenly, sales started taking off, and it all had to do with product knowledge."

Financial institutions add value to their services with expertise in their service. Expertise is an inescapable requirement of financial service excellence. Service providers who possess job-specific technical skills and knowledge and who also possess the communication skills to effectively transmit that knowledge to customers and prospects are positioned to deliver excellent service and meet or exceed the expectations of customers and prospects.

What Backroom Staff Needs

Generally, the skills training described for direct contact personnel applies to backroom staff as well. Elaborating on the fact that "everybody has a customer," a consultant with considerable experience in service quality training and education explains that good communication skills and the ability to understand and apply the dimensions of service are as appropriate to encounters with internal customers as they are to external service situations.

"The biggest difference," she says, "is that operations and support people don't always recognize the connection. It's an attitude or awareness problem. Including them in the same classes or workshops as direct contact personnel is valuable because it helps instill a sense of teamwork, and underlines that the accuracy and thoroughness of their contribution can make the difference between a satisfied customer and one who breaks off the relationship."

We strongly endorse the idea of including backroom and direct contact personnel in the same training and education programs whenever possible. More generally, we advocate programs that foster awareness of what transpires in other functional areas of the institution, especially those that are closely connected to a given work group. Team building in a given work unit is relatively simple; developing an interdepartmental sense of teamwork is more difficult, but equally important to an organization's overall service quality effort.

Barclays Bank, London, demonstrates the team-building approach, starting from the top down. "In the early stages, our training program covered nearly all staff, from Regional Directors downward, in a series of two-day training courses," C. J. Lendrum says. "Following that we educated all customer service staff, with 71,000 people going through 4,700 courses.

A lot of the training has been done on what we call a 'diagonal slice' basis, so that we're not just training all the cashiers together and all the securities people together. Instead, we're training managers, cashiers, and securities people together in groups, so that they can react to each other during the training program."

Bringing direct contact personnel into the "backshop" and operations personnel into the "frontshop" so that related work groups can better understand each other's requirements and reality is money well spent. It is difficult for backshop personnel to be sufficiently sensitive to the expectations of frontshop personnel—or to be zealous about meeting those expectations—if they never lay eyes on those people, never meet them, never even hear from them unless they are complaining.

Backroom service providers need the job-critical technical skills to be efficient and reliable in their work. They also need communication skill training—especially those having regular contact with internal or external customers by telephone or mail. They also need knowledge. They need the knowledge that beyond the bank of telephones or computers or check-processing machines that they see everyday is a service-selling-and-delivery system of people, processes, machines, and facilities dependent on the services they themselves provide. Backroom service providers need to be aware of this broader system of which they are an integral part. They need to understand that they, too, have customers to serve, and they need the opportunity to know these customers and learn their expectations.

WHAT HAPPENS WHEN THE CLASSROOM LIGHTS GO OUT?

For training and education to "take" and truly effect behavioral change, it must be reinforced in its aftermath. One banker cautions, "We can send the line service providers to training session after training session, but it will be a waste of time unless the proper environment is created by the line manager back at the work area."

Middle managers, as we have said, are the key. They set

the tone in the immediate work environment. If they are unsupportive, much of the training and education investment made will go down the drain. One major bank we know spends large sums of money teaching its branch managers to "coach" platform personnel to sell. A year after the program was started they hired a consultant to find out why some branches' cross-sell ratios had not increased. The consultant discovered that several of the managers had never even taken the shrinkwrap off the coaching feedback forms!

Nothing puts more of a damper on new skills and enthusiasm stemming from a training/education experience than facing a supervisor who shows no interest in the application of the skills and who disallows any opportunity to use them. One author summarizes the problem,[7] "If employees don't get the time necessary to use their quality training, they forget most of what they learned in quality classes. Managers wonder why employees are not using the skills they were taught. And this leads to more training, reduced time to meet production, nonuse of learned quality skills, no quality improvement, more training, etc.—a vicious circle. It isn't that employees don't care about improving quality. Unless they are given time to hone their quality improvement skills, those skills will never really be mastered and quality will stagnate."

Managers need to know the content of skill and knowledge development programs in order to support and encourage behavior changes on the job, a fact that generally requires that managers take these programs first. Training and education for managers is truly pivotal—for the example it sets, for the understanding it builds, and for the leadership and coaching skills it nurtures.

Team meetings provide a prime opportunity for reinforcing skills that have been taught and for upgrading relevant knowledge. Many skill and knowledge development programs are structured as initial sessions, to be followed by additional sessions 3, 6, or 12 months later. Regular team meetings provide team members with an opportunity to brush up on skills and knowledge, receive additional training and education, solve service problems, have fun, and experience the sense of "we are all in this together."

One banker surveyed notes that reinforcement in his organization includes a "formalized awareness program," requiring that 50 percent of all employee communication directly concern quality service. Another banker adds, "We get people to reflect on how they were affected by poor service at a department store or restaurant, and then ask them what they did because of that service. That leads to a discussion of how to avoid negative encounters with our customers."

Techniques to reinforce service awareness are limited only by the imagination. At the Meridian Banking Group, employees attempt to fill out deposit slips with Vaseline smeared on their glasses or to count money with three fingers on each hand taped together. The idea is to help them understand the problems that older customers with glaucoma or arthritis may face in the bank.[8]

USE A VARIETY OF APPROACHES

There is no single training and education methodology that covers all needs. We recommend the use of multiple approaches to service skill and knowledge development. Following are several widely used approaches to training and education; many organizations combine them all, and add others besides:

Self-Instructional Programming
Self-instructional programming through manuals, workbooks, videotapes, computers, or other means is particularly appropriate to develop job-related skills that follow a logical sequence of steps. Advantages include uniformity of the training regimen, the opportunity to work through the materials at one's own pace, and the ability to offer programming as needed, rather than having to wait for enough people to fill a class. One potential pitfall is not providing assistance to employees who need help with the material. Many organizations solve this problem by bringing trainees together in a classroom situation at regular intervals or assigning them a mentor to answer questions.

Classroom Presentations
Classroom situations offer the opportunity for group discussions, and provide a forum for executives from different parts of

the organization to address the group on various facets of the subject being studied. Programming that brings employees together as a group is critical in facilitating a "synergy" of ideas, establishing common understanding, and building a sense of teamwork.

Role-Playing

Mastery of the communication skills and product knowledge needed for service excellence requires practice. Role-playing service interactions allows employees the opportunity to test and practice service skills and knowledge and get feedback from those observing.

"Shopping"

Playing the role of customer in actual service encounters can give service providers insight into the customer's reality that they can't get any other way. Shopping takes the practice of role-playing one step further by placing employees in the "real life" situation of experiencing from others the services they themselves provide. As one banker comments, "It can be an eye-opening experience." Bringing employees back together as a group to discuss their shopping experiences can be especially powerful.

Videotapes

In addition to providing a break in the rhythm of classroom/ lecture programs, videotaped segments allow the same material to be reused. Possibilities include videotaped role-playing, case studies customer focus group interviews for group analysis and discussion, and important presentations by guest lecturers who are not always available when needed to restate the material. Videotapes are also a valuable tool for management to use to reinforce the service message.

Cross-Fertilization

Many executives from a variety of industries make a practice of seeing what life is like in the line of fire, both for the education it provides and to make their own commitment to service quality more visible throughout the organization. Thomas M. Bloch, President of Tax Operations for H & R Block, attempts to spend at least 2 days every month in a tax office doing the job of a tax preparer or receptionist. He also spends at least 1 day during the tax season in the customer service department, handling customer complaints. Bloch explains, "There is a big difference between watching a job done and doing it yourself. It helps top managers stay close to the business and encourages all managers to do the same." Cross-fertilization need not be restricted to executives, although it is particularly critical that decision makers directly experience the realities of the service delivery system. Cross-fertilization is healthy at any organizational level.

The best way to insure that skill and knowledge development is ongoing—a process, not an event—is to rely on multiple concepts: group and individual learning, centralized and decentralized learning, learning by hearing and learning by doing, learning one's own job, and learning other people's jobs as well. The mix of approaches enumerated above, plus others referred to earlier such as one-on-one coaching and regular team meetings, conveys our philosophy of using a portfolio of methods and keeping the train running.

SHOULD INSTITUTIONS MAKE OR BUY?

A financial institution should try to develop at least some of its own service quality training and education materials. Service quality skills and knowledge development is too important an issue—and too closely tied to an institution's unique requirements—to be left entirely in the hands of outsiders. In addition, the steady, ongoing reinforcement that service quality training and education requires is most likely to occur if the institution retains control over what is taught and when.

On the other hand, a subject area as complex and multi-faceted as service quality requires expertise that may not be fully available in an organization. Producing materials also can be a costly and time-consuming process. Consultants can also provide an objective point of view that might be lacking internally.

If a consultant is to be used, it pays to look for one who will tailor appropriate materials to meet the unique needs of the client institution. It also pays to use a consultant whose orientation is to help the client develop sufficient in-house capability so that outside services will be less and less necessary.

EVALUATING SKILL AND KNOWLEDGE DEVELOPMENT

Just as introducing training and educational programs without first assessing the need for them is a mistake, so is it a mistake to provide these programs without evaluating results. Are instructors effective in imparting the material? Are the methods optimum? Are employees using the skills and knowledge being taught? Do managers notice a difference in employee attitudes and behavior? Do customers? Is service quality getting better?

We recommend a multistage evaluation of skill and knowledge development efforts. How do employees rate the course and instructor immediately after its completion? How do they rate the experience after 30 or 60 days? What new skills or knowledge are they actually using? What skills and knowledge aren't they using—and why?

Ongoing evaluation of training and education programs gives an institution the opportunity to learn from its experiences, correct its mistakes, fine-tune its methods, and assess the impact and value of its investment. It is an important thing to do.

MAKE THE MOST OF YOUR TRAINING AND EDUCATION INVESTMENT

Throughout this chapter, we have stressed that training and education is a process, not an event. Without continual skill and knowledge upgrading and reinforcement, the service quality journey is destined to stall.

The existing culture in an organization can create massive inertia. Often the challenge is to "undo" the old to make way for the new. Training and education are among the most powerful tools for achieving excellence. But the moment management lets its attention wander and relaxes its grip on the wheel, momentum will likely falter. Indeed, that is what some will be waiting for—any indication that the "focus on service quality" is just another program, just another event.

Don't let that happen! Tie skill and knowledge development and the changes it encourages to larger corporate issues. Listen to Chase Manhattan Vice President Ronald Koprowski when he says, "Our training programs relate the purpose of the program to our overall vision and mission statements, as well as to our key strategic thrusts in the business."

In closing, we leave you with these suggestions for making the most of your training and education investment:

- Start with a needs analysis, and use the results.
- Start new service quality training and education initiatives with visible kick-offs involving senior management.
- Insist that service quality materials be integrated into every skill and knowledge development offering in the institution.
- Implement from the top down, and make sure each group communicates what went on at the previous upper level sessions.
- Ask line managers to lead training and educational programs, especially for other managers.
- Build momentum and enthusiasm by starting rollouts in parts of the institution that are most likely to succeed.
- Build training and educational opportunities into regular sales and service meetings.
- Include exercises that encourage employees to use their own service quality experiences.
- Use a rich portfolio of training and education approaches.
- Evaluate continuously and comprehensively.
- Use training and educational opportunities to develop a sense of "team."
- Make training and education fun. Try looking at the world through Vaseline-covered glasses!

NOTES

1. "Do You Know Me?" *Business Week,* January 25, 1988, p. 79.
2. Kahn, Joseph P., and Pearlstein, Steven. "Merchant Prince Stanley Marcus," *Inc.,* June, 1987, p. 48.
3. Mager, Robert F., and Pipe, Peter. *Analyzing Performance Problems.* Belmont, CA: Pitman Learning, Inc., 1970.
4. Ibid., p. 2.
5. Hennessey, Paul, Deden, Ann, and Rochwarger, Michelle. "The Branch Manager: Key to Retail Sales Performance." *Journal of Retail Banking,* Summer 1985.
6. Berry, Leonard L. "Communication Central to Customer Service." *American Banker,* March 11, 1987.
7. Brown, Mark G. "Bridging the Quality Gap." *Quality,* June 1987, p. 44.
8. Bacas, Harry. "Make It Right for the Customer." *Nation's Business,* November 1987.

CHAPTER 9

REINFORCING HIGH
QUALITY SERVICE

When you get recognized for doing good, it makes you go for it.
—*A bank customer service representative*

Service performance is influenced strongly by three factors: the skills and knowledge an individual brings to the job, the skills and knowledge an individual develops on the job, and an individual's motivation for performing the job. We described the first factor in Chapter 7 in the section on "selection." We discussed the second in Chapter 8 on "preparing people to serve." We are now ready to discuss the third factor—the mysterious, elusive, and all-powerful concept of motivation.

An individual's motivation to perform the service is a critical factor in the pursuit of service excellence because motivation is often the *only* difference between mediocre and outstanding service and even mediocre and disastrous service. One needs only to reflect back on the banker who helped the customer find the hospital (Chapter 8) and Lottye Carlin's credit card disaster (Chapter 7) to see the crucial difference between truly inspired service and "going through the motions" service. In both situations, individual service providers had the opportunity to do something "extra" to help a customer in need. In the former situation, the opportunity was met and a banking relationship was strengthened. In the latter case, the opportunity was missed repeatedly and the final tab included nationwide negative publicity and a settlement of $150,000. Motivation, desire, willingness to perform—choose your own label—was present in the first case and absent in the second. It is as simple—and as complicated—as that!

The individual employee's willingness to do the "extras," to do the little things, to add a touch of grace to the service, is influenced directly by the organizational culture in which the employee functions. Culture, after all, defines what is important, what is valued in the organization. How can we expect even the most self-motivated individuals to try extra hard for customers day after day and week after week if the organization does not respond to this behavior, if no one in the organizational hierarchy seems to notice—or care?

But what are the keys to culture? We have answered this question only partially at this point in the book. Certainly, service-minded leadership at all levels of the organization is a key. The types of research done and how the research is used are also important. So are organizational structure, employee selection practices, and skill and knowledge development programming.

Having discussed these and other culture-shaping influences, we now complete the service puzzle with a discussion of the service quality mini-loop: service standards, service performance measurement, and service rewards. The service quality mini-loop, shown in Figure 9–1, is at the heart of the culture-building process. Employees realize something is really important if management defines it as a work priority (standards), keeps score (performance measurement), and recognizes those who perform the best (rewards). When management does all of this, when it closes the mini-loop, it sends a powerful message throughout the organization. The message is: service excellence matters, service excellence is "winning" behavior. As Edgar Schein writes:[1]

> Members of any organization learn from their own experience with promotions, performance appraisals, and discussions with the boss what the organization values and punishes. Both the nature of the behavior rewarded and punished and the nature of the rewards and punishments themselves carry the messages. An organization's leaders can quickly get across their own priorities, values, and assumptions by consistently linking rewards and punishments to the behavior they are concerned with.

FIGURE 9–1
The Service Quality Mini-Loop

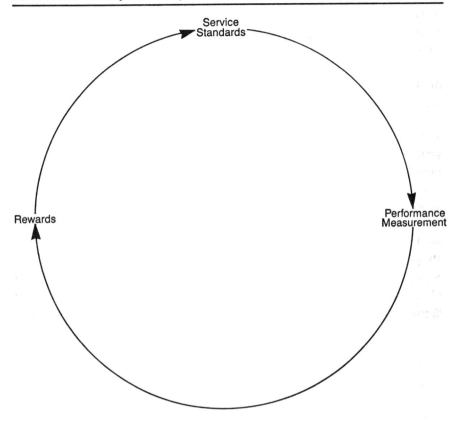

SETTING AND COMMUNICATING
SERVICE STANDARDS

Two essential factors are critical to setting standards. First, service standards *must* be research-based because they will be dysfunctional unless they reflect customers' most important expectations. If service standards are based on assumption—and are incorrect—they will lead employees astray, causing them to overlook or de-emphasize the most essential service performance dimensions.

Second, the setting of service standards should precede major new investments in service skill and knowledge development. The heart of training and education for service quality is to give service providers the skill, knowledge, and inspiration to meet or exceed service standards. Thus, in laying the groundwork for building a service-minded culture in an organization, it is appropriate to discuss the concept of service standards (Chapter 6) before addressing the concept of skill and knowledge development (Chapter 8).

Now we return to the subject of service standards, but with a different slant. The focus of our discussion will detail the link among service standards, performance measurement, and reward systems.

The primary role of service standards is to present customer expectations in a language that service providers understand and find meaningful. Service standards not only clarify service roles and convey priorities for individual employees, they also provide "benchmarks" against which individual and institutional performance can be measured. When an organization establishes explicit service performance standards, it then knows what performance to measure. And when an organization does a good job of performance measurement, it is relatively easy to identify those service providers who deserve to be rewarded. Closing the mini-loop of service quality boosts "role clarity," a prime motivator.[2]

Establishing service standards is only half of the challenge. Equally important is communicating these standards. If service providers are unsure of the standards by which they will be judged in the organization, or if they do not take them seriously because the standards are rarely mentioned and reinforced, the behavior-guiding and motivational benefits of service standards are lost.

MBank in Houston, Texas, launched "First MPressions" in 1987 based on a series of courtesy standards for all internal and external service encounters. These standards, some of which appear in Figure 9–2, are incorporated into job descriptions, included in the employee orientation program, reprinted on laminated prompter cards, monitored through an ongoing "mystery shopper" program, and built into the supervision and reward process.

FIGURE 9–2
Courtesy Standards at MBank*

- *Smile sincerely* and make eye contact when you greet customers. Don't avert your eyes or look down when a customer approaches you. Say "Hello," "How are you," and "May I help you" in a friendly way.
- *Introduce yourself* either when the customer first walks up or immediately when you answer the telephone.
- *Use the customer's name twice.* In many instances, you will have the customer's name right in front of you—on a deposit slip check, or on the CRT —so use it. It makes the customer feel important.
- *Give the customer your undivided attention.* When you're talking to a customer, put aside the papers at your desk, quit adding up a column of numbers or writing a report.
- *Answer questions accurately and completely.* Don't guess. If you're not sure of the answer, check with someone who knows and get back to the customer immediately.
- *Refer the customer to another MBanker by introducing the customer and explaining the situation.* If the customer is in the bank, call ahead to the person who you are referring them to.
- *Give specific directions to other areas of the bank.* Say, "The Personal Banking Center is in the southwest corner of the first floor across from Customer Service"—rather than "on the first floor."
- *Say "Please" and "Thank You."*

*Reprinted by permission of MBank. A separate set of standards has been developed for telephone encounters.

We advise financial institutions to use every reasonable opportunity to communicate and reinforce service standards, including continual reference to them in meetings and training/education sessions, reproducing them in internal media such as wallet cards, desk signs, posters and house organs, and linking them specifically to performance measurement, appraisals, and rewards.

The first priority for service standards is to specify desired behavior patterns for service providers. "If employees know what is expected, then they can learn and improve," says Nancy S. Major, Vice President and Director of Service Management, First Union National Bank, Charlotte, North Carolina.[3] However, standards serve another purpose as well. Because they guide the performance of service providers, standards also serve as a control mechanism for management. They are the basis for evaluating the performance of individual employees and work units against customer expectations, for tracking the development of the organization's service culture, and for identifying problems that may require additional training, education, or other corrective action.

MEASURING SERVICE PERFORMANCE

Performance measurement is the second element in the service quality mini-loop. Service standards will be rendered meaningless unless performance against the standards is measured.

Service providers need to know how they are doing. They also need to know that others in the organization will be aware of their performance. Finally, they need to know that their individual performance makes a difference. A well-conceived performance measurement system will deliver on each of these requirements: feedback for service providers, dissemination of results to key "others" in the organization, and an equitable basis for a reward system.

Performance measurement is highly symbolic. People working in organizations quickly figure out what is most important to management by noting the types of performance that management measures. It is clear to all that management "keeps score" on the important things. Thus, when a financial institution measures branch managers on expense control but not on branch service ratings, it sends out cultural signals that a ton of management rhetoric about the importance of service will not diminish.

The most familiar type of performance measurement is "output" measurement that centers on results, for example, the number of customers processed per time period, the number of sales made per customer. However, the use of "outputs" is often inappropriate or insufficient to measure service performance. For example, measuring teller performance strictly on the basis of such outputs as end-of-the-day balancing excludes key service dimensions such as assurance and empathy.[4]

What are needed are measures that focus on behavior

during service delivery. The use of a "behavioral" measure was illustrated in Chapter 6 in the discussion of Friendly Bank's "tone-of-service" survey in which customers answer questions about the service provider's behavior soon after service is rendered. Friendly Bank also measures contact personnel performance through ongoing "shopper" research (another behavioral measure) and through a cross-selling index (an output measure). Friendly Bank's use of an appropriate mix of behavioral and output measures encourages service performance that is consistent with customer expectations.[5]

Use Customer Input

Service performance measurement, by definition, must be based on customer input. As we have stressed throughout this book, customer perceptions of quality are the only perceptions that count! A service performance measurement system that does not incorporate customer feedback is inherently flawed. One banker makes the point when telling of a conversation he had with bank personnel who had developed a customer complaint tracking system:

> They told me they had a very good system that allowed us to track what customers called in about—whether it was a complaint or just an inquiry, how it was resolved, and how long it took us to resolve it. And I asked, "How do we know it was resolved? Who enters data?" The reply was that the customer service officer tells us it was resolved. And I said, "Is there any way for *customers* to tell us it was resolved, because it's not resolved until they're happy."
>
> The thing that concerns me most is that this whole system was developed for our internal needs, and no one had really thought about getting a handle on what the customer was thinking. When I have the systems people come to me and say, "Not only do we have this system, but we've talked with customers, and we've designed it this way," or when I hear management saying, "We've made this decision because the customer has told us to take this position"—that's when we've achieved service quality. Measurement is in their eyes, not mine.

The use of customer input is just as essential in measuring the service performance of "backshop" service providers as it is in measuring the performance of "frontshop" providers. At First American National Bank in Nashville, branch employees are asked to grade the service performance of the Operations and Information Systems Division on 102 services provided to the branches. The Division asks branch personnel to complete "report cards" using an A, B, C, D, and F grading system. The Division then follows up with the branches on corrective actions taken for services that received poor grades.

Measure Individual and Group Performance

The ideal service performance measurement system will capture data at the individual employee level and will also provide for the aggregation of data at the operating unit level. The very best way to encourage individual accountability for service quality is to measure service performance at the individual employee level. What can play more into the hands of poor service providers than the absence of individual performance measurement? What can be more demoralizing to outstanding service providers than for no one in management to notice their excellence? Individual service performance measurement is essential!

Service performance measurement at the work unit level is also valuable in that it invites comparisons among similar organizational groups and can spur healthy competition among these groups. Group measurement can also unleash peer pressure, perhaps the most powerful of all motivators.

To be sure, these favorable outcomes of group measurement are no sure thing. Group service scores will need to be publicized in the organization and tied to the reward system. Moreover, there is a fine line between healthy and unhealthy competition within the organization, between positive peer pressure that is motivating and negative peer pressure that is intimidating.

The more positive the measurement approaches, the reward systems, and the overall tone of supervisory leadership, the more likely it is that group measurement will lead to favor-

FIGURE 9–3
Measuring Individual and Group Service Performance

Research Approaches	Level of Data Aggregation	
	Individual Worker	Work Group
Expectation and Perception Surveys		X
Tone of Service Surveys	X	X
Shopper Research	X	X
Complaint Solicitation		X

able consequences. It is impossible to build a strong service culture through intimidation and fear.

Measuring the service performance of individuals and groups can be done using, among other approaches, the research approaches discussed in Chapter 6. Data from tone-of-service and shopper research on individual performance can be averaged for specific work units. Data from expectation and perception surveys and complaint solicitation research can also be broken down by work units. Figure 9–3 illustrates these concepts.

Build a System that Is Fair

Fairness is one of the most important criteria to consider in designing a service performance measurement system. An unfair system is a bad system, period!

Importantly, the system must not only be fair, it must be perceived as fair. If employees perceive the measurements to be unfair, they will not trust the feedback the system brings, they will resent the dissemination of the data (especially when unfavorable), and they will consider the reward system to be flawed.

A measurement system characterized by the following is most likely to be perceived as fair:

- The measures relate directly to service standards. There is maximum consistency between the priorities of a service role and the manner in which role performance is measured.
- Service providers are prepared to perform the service role. They have been given the opportunity to learn the skills and knowledge they need to do well in the measurement system.
- Service providers have provided input on the appropriateness and fairness of the measures that are used.
- The measurement approaches have been explained to those whose performance is being measured. The "rules of the game" are clear to all involved.
- The measures are administered on an ongoing basis to minimize the impact of a single measurement encounter. The system accommodates the "bad days" that even the finest service providers will have.
- The measures are as uniform as possible among work groups so that everyone "plays by the same rules."
- Multiple approaches are used to overcome the disadvantages of any one approach and to provide different-angled views of service performance.

Several of these criteria are evident in the multiple-method approach to evaluating branch service quality that is used at Security Pacific National Bank in California. In this system, branch managers receive a monthly report on their branch's service performance. Methodologies include customer surveys, in-person and telephone shoppers, and interviews and observations by bank quality assurance officers. A typical monthly rating for a branch is based on a combination of reports from in-branch shoppers, telephone shoppers, and a visit by a quality assurance officer.

"You need to use multiple techniques to afford yourself all the different comparisons you can," states Security Pacific's Richard Davis. "The only thing I promise is that every banking office will be judged using the same yardstick, and that the techniques have been purified to assure they are as credible as possible. I also promise that the resulting feedback will be in terms of the standards and determinants that have been communicated to them. There are no secrets."

Once a month, banking office service delivery is observed and management interviewed by quality assurance officers who factor into their assessments salient conditions within a given branch, for example, lower than normal staffing. These branch visits are a powerful tool according to Davis. He states:

> Not only can I deliver information, I can also capture any data that I might want. If top management says, "I've got to know what people in the system are feeling about this," or, "I have to know if we're doing that," I can provide the answer by making sure that personnel in 40 offices have been interviewed by the end of the day. That's power that I don't know we've ever had before. It's a lot better than telephones, and more candid as well.

Mystery shoppers, on the other hand, offer a customer perspective that the observational techniques of the quality assurance officers do not provide. "However, shoppers don't have the same understanding that my people do in terms of what we're requiring from branch personnel, such as what collateral material they are supposed to be showing, and what kinds of sales aids they have been taught to use," Davis says. "Mystery shoppers are looking at it from a whole different perspective, and I love it because we're capturing multiple perspectives as we do that—none of them wrong, yet none of them standing alone."

People Want to Know

People at work want feedback. They want to know how they are doing. Accordingly, it is very important not only to measure service performance well, but to actually use these data in supervisory coaching, feedback sessions, performance appraisals, and, of course, in reward decisions.

When performance feedback is shared with service providers in a timely and constructive manner, it can be a source of new energy and stimulation. Carl Sewell, CEO of Sewell Village Cadillac in Dallas and other automobile dealerships, tells the story of how Sewell Village "lot lizards" significantly improved their performance. "Lot lizard" is a phrase commonly used to refer to dealership employees who deliver just-serviced cars from the parking lot to the waiting customer. The first thing Sewell did was change the name of the position to "customer service representative" to convey a more professional image. Next, he installed a computerized system that informed the customer service representative which car should be brought from the lot. This system also automatically tracked the time it took to deliver the car to the customer, information that was not initially shared with the customer service representatives. Then, after a request from a customer service representative, the information was made available. The result was that the average elapsed delivery time quickly dropped from four and one-half minutes to two minutes.

The lesson was not lost on Carl Sewell, generally considered to be one of America's most customer-minded automobile dealers. He says, "We measure everything we can think of in the dealership, and we share everything we measure."

Measuring service performance well helps to fuel the service quality journey. It gives "teeth" to service standards and provides the *only* basis for an effective reward system. It requires the same rigor and objectivity that companies routinely bring to issues of productivity, costs, and revenues. It requires quantifying customer care.[6]

REWARDING SERVICE EXCELLENCE

Whereas a well-executed performance measurement system will get employee attention, a well-executed reward system will help keep it. As one banker comments, "People are our major asset. We have to keep them motivated, and rewarding performance is the most powerful way of doing it." Indeed, nothing underlines an organization's commitment to service quality as much as management's willingness to pay for it.

Designing and implementing an effective system for rewarding service excellence is easy. The often heard notion that reward systems are tricky or difficult to administer is nonsense. What is tricky is developing an effective performance measurement system that is tied to explicit service standards for every type of service position in the organization. Once such a system is in place, it will identify the individuals and work groups delivering the most outstanding service, making the rewarding process itself quite simple. Where many attempted reward programs go astray is that they are not supported with good information on who deserves and doesn't deserve to be rewarded. Doling out rewards based on political considerations or otherwise ineffectual criteria is what dooms many attempted reward initiatives to failure.

We strongly believe that all service providers should be expected to meet the service standards established for their positions. This is their job, and if they cannot do the job they should not remain in it. Special rewards should be reserved for those service providers who provide outstanding service, service providers who consistently exceed service standards and who demonstrate a commitment to customer care that sets an example for others to follow.

Reward systems should accentuate the positive. Underlying reinforcers for service excellence—inspiration, teamwork, open and honest communications, belief in the company, among others—are far more likely when the emphasis is on rewarding outstanding performance, rather than punishing poor performance. Even with poor performers, the emphasis should generally be on constructive feedback, coaching, additional skills and knowledge development, and/or other indicated interventions. If these fail, then the poor performers need to leave the position, rather than stay in it and be "punished."

The most effective reward systems involve a reward triangle: direct financial rewards, career advancement, and nonfinancial recognition.[7] Financial institution executives who truly wish to keep their employees' attention riveted to service excellence will want to build a reward system that incorporates all three approaches for individuals *and* work groups. Figure 9–4 illustrates the reward triangle.

Direct Financial Awards

Monetary rewards in the form of salary increases, bonuses, on-the-spot payouts, contests, and other methods can be a potent force for changing performance behavior—and sustaining that change. However, the power of pay as a reward is very much related to the rationale and manner with which it is used. If

FIGURE 9–4
The Reward Triangle

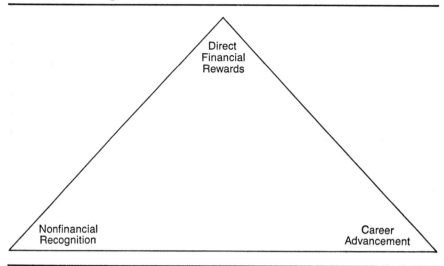

Source: Leonard L Berry, Charles M. Futrell, and Michael Bowers. *Bankers Who Sell—Improving Selling Effectiveness in Banking.* Chicago: Bank Marketing Association, and Homewood, IL: Dow Jones-Irwin, 1985, p. 120.

employees are confused about how service performance affects their income, if they receive regular merit raises without improving their level of service, or if they think others in the organization receive higher compensation for the same performance behaviors, financial rewards are unlikely to have the desired effect. Financial (and other) rewards have the most impact when they reflect actual performance.

Effective financial rewards for service excellence should be built into the regular performance appraisal/merit raise cycle. It is very important that service performance be stressed when managers discuss the rationale for pay raises with subordinates.

Merit pay raises for service excellence do not go far enough, however. Annual or semi-annual merit raises related to service performance are necessary, but they often occur well after the behaviors they are designed to reward. More timely rewards that stimulate day-to-day behavior, convey feedback on performance, and help deepen the organization's service culture are equally important.

Monetary rewards need not be large. The point is *doing it,* making the effort to recognize the most excellent service providers. For many employees, the most valued part of a monetary reward is not what they can buy with the extra funds but rather that management has noticed their work and likes what they see.

The possibilities for effective financial reward systems are unlimited. Management commitment, imagination, and a good performance measurement system tied to service standards are the key elements.

At United Bank of Denver, "each department has a service incentive budget, and managers develop programs which they believe will work for their department," says Executive Vice President Beverly Haddon. "They have monthly cash awards, put some extra money in the vacation pot, take people out to lunch, and give away tickets to sporting events. Quarterly awards are distributed by me or the manager who reports to me, so there is recognition from senior management as well."

At First Union National Bank of North Carolina, 20 percent of the branch managers' incentive pay is based on the branch's Quality Customer Service (QCS) scores, which are determined from shoppers by an outside firm. Branch personnel can earn as much for a perfect QCS shopping session as for any single service they might sell, and tellers earn bonus incentive points for superior QCS scores during shopping sessions.[8]

At First Interstate Bank of Arizona, mystery shopping is used extensively to reward excellent service providers. Executive Vice President F. Harlan Loffman explains:

> We started a Teller Appreciation Program. We asked our tellers to do five things when waiting on their customers: smile, greet the customer, establish eye contact, call the customer by name, and thank the customer for his or her business. Anonymous shoppers were trained and sent to our branches. If a teller did all five of the above, the shopper immediately called over the teller's supervisor and awarded the teller $10 and a recognition certificate. The percentage of tellers winning more than doubled in the first year. The program works because the reward is im-

mediate, the teller's supervisor is involved, and the incentive is appropriate. Tellers like the immediate cash, and the certificate gives them a more permanent type of recognition for their achievement. We also publicize the program heavily, and surround it with a great deal of hoopla.

One of the most interesting reward programs we have come across is the President's Special Quality Award Program started by John Creedon, President and CEO of Metropolitan Life Insurance Company. Started in 1986, the initial program involved 1,000 awards of $1,000 each to Metropolitan employees who demonstrated "an obsession with quality" in serving their customers. The program was kept simple, with no forms to complete or burdensome procedures to follow. Customers and employees could nominate individuals for the awards simply by writing a letter of nomination to the president. Both internal and external service providers were eligible for the awards. Selection was made on the basis of the nomination letter and consultation with managers familiar with a nominee's performance. The awards were presented by local management, who were encouraged to use the occasions to promote departmental quality improvement efforts. The program was continued after the first 1,000 awards were made; as of April, 1988, more than 1,400 awards had been given.

Career Advancement

Making service performance a principal factor in promotion decisions is one of the strongest statements that management can make about the importance of service. What is crucial is that employees perceive a career stake in providing excellent service. The best service providers not only need to progress more rapidly in their careers than others, they and their peers need to perceive that service performance is a principal reason why. Paying outstanding servers more *and* promoting them more quickly represent a powerful one-two combination. Add nonfinancial recognition to the mix, and the personal value of striving for excellence becomes unmistakable.

Successfully linking career advancement to service performance requires several doses of nontraditional thinking. For one thing, it is important to communicate internally who is receiving promotions and why. Quiet is not the ticket; the connection between service and success needs to be marketed.

Also, organizations need to overcome the common problems of limited promotion opportunities and promoting people out of their realm of competence. Not only might there be limited opportunities to promote, say, outstanding customer service representatives, but also some of these individuals may not make good supervisors, an otherwise logical promotion step.

What to do? We recommend that financial institutions develop explicit career paths that involve two kinds of promotional ladders. One ladder would be within given positions (such as customer service representative), and the second ladder would connect different positions. Thus, a financial institution might have four levels of customer service representatives, with each succeeding level involving more skill and knowledge development opportunities, more income potential, and broader responsibilities. To properly implement a dual-ladder program, financial institution executives will have to reconsider salary classification systems that "cap" income potential once an employee has advanced several grades. As an experienced bank customer service representative once asked one of the authors, "Why can't they reward my success with more money, rather than me having to change my job?"[9]

Nonfinancial Recognition

They appear on the cover and page after page of Norwest Corporation's 1987 Annual Report: full-color photographs of employees who have distinguished themselves through sales and service excellence. They are members of the company's "100 Percent Club" and "Service Excellence Club." And although an incentive gift program and year-end drawing for vacation cruises were involved, recognition for its own sake was the point of both programs, according to Marketing Officer Christy J. Blake.

"Both programs—the 100 Percent Club for salespeople

and the Service Excellence Club for support staff—were initiated a year ago as motivational tools by senior management," Blake explains. "Before establishing the programs, we asked our employees what it would take to improve sales and service. We received many suggestions, but one that stood out was that people felt they weren't being recognized for a job well done."

What Norwest employees said they wanted was a "good pat on the back." If they were winners, they wanted everyone to know why they'd won. "People felt that receiving a plaque and a handshake in front of their peers was a motivating thing," Blake said. "And it works. As a result of the program, both service and salespeople tend to be more responsive, especially if someone in the same department has won an award. It's an effective motivational tool because it lets people know their work is noticed by management and their peers."

Norwest Corporation found out what kind of recognition employees valued by asking them. And what they found out is that people love a parade! What they continue to discover is the power of nonmonetary recognition to energize and sustain the bank's service and sales focus. Recognition lets people know that they are part of the team, that they are valued.

It is hard to overstate the motivational impact of well-conceived, sincere recognition. If viewed as a supplement to the other elements of the reward triangle (rather than as a replacement) and if reserved for outstanding service performers (rather than used carelessly), nonfinancial recognitions will repay in increased employee motivation, spirit, and goodwill far more than they cost.

Many of the executives we surveyed understand the importance of nonfinancial recognition for service excellence and use a variety of means to bestow it. For example:

- A "highly visible" 5-foot-tall trophy, awarded each quarter to the bank's top performing branch. "It's not enough for the staff to know they offer the best service in the system," a bank executive comments. "They want their customers to know it, too."
- Monthly "Quality Assurance" awards for operations center employees. Once a month, service center employ-

ees take a 20-minute break and come to a central area in the facility to see the winners receive plaques from management. Monthly winners then compete for annual awards given by the chairman of the bank.

- A "Quality Touch Club"—a bankwide, peer nomination process that recognizes individuals delivering excellent service to both internal and external customers. Nominees' qualifications are evaluated and reviewed monthly by a committee. Inductees are honored at a luncheon hosted by the district president and receive personalized, engraved awards. Inductees' photographs are displayed in their branches or departments for a month and then added to the "wall of fame" in district main offices. Inductees' biographies are included in the bank newsletter.

- A "Star Quality Program" for internal and external service providers. Employees whose service is complimented by customers in writing or verbally to a supervisor are eligible for the "Gold Star" award. Presentations are made at "Star Quality" breakfasts, which are attended by senior management and the employees' supervisors.

Celebrations of service excellence do not have to be big events. Tom Peters stresses the importance of small actions to let people know their daily efforts are being noticed and are appreciated—picking up a dozen doughnuts on the way to work to celebrate a project completed on deadline; holding an inexpensive, in-office lunch party to honor a work group or individual; sending handwritten thank-you notes; and giving out trinkets or small gifts, for example, coffee mugs or belt buckles.[10]

It is easy for service providers to be demoralized by the rigors of the daily grind. Service quality "parades"—both big extravaganzas and small impromptu events—help give meaning to the routine of service work, and are an effective means of recharging workers' "batteries." They give tangible recognition to top performers and, at the same time, encourage others to improve. They reinforce teamwork and humanize supervisors who participate in the festivities. Finally, parades are fun, and

FIGURE 9–5
Guidelines for Formal Service Celebrations

- Choose a theme that identifies and anchors the celebration.
- Include "grass-roots" leaders as well as managerial level service champions in the planning, and work together to develop a program that has vitality, variety, and sincerity.
- Create a festive environment—balloons, colorful decorations, and special lighting.
- Honor a diverse and numerous group to show that service quality is broadly accepted within the institution and that it takes a variety of service providers to make up the team.
- Give "hardware"—plaques, trophies, desk accessories, special calling cards, briefcases, or other tangible symbols of merit.
- Provide inexpensive remembrances for everyone, such as programs or small table prizes.
- Make sure a photographer is in attendance to take photos for company publications, posting on office bulletin boards, or for personal momentos.
- Schedule time for socializing before and after the main event to savor the moment and provide an opportunity for "family" talk.
- Invite senior executives to participate in the festivities.

Source: Leonard L. Berry and George A. Rieder. "Parade Is Festive Way to Honor Service Workers." *American Banker*, December 31, 1987.

fun is important in difficult jobs![11] Some guidelines for planning more formal service celebrations appear in Figure 9–5.

SUSTAINING THE SERVICE CULTURE

Sustaining the momentum of a service culture—keeping the organization from stalling on the service quality journey—is one of management's biggest challenges. It requires constant attention and vigilance. The search for ways to improve service must be ongoing. Intraorganizational and interorganizational communication and team-building must be ongoing. Skill and knowledge development must be ongoing. And so must efforts to establish and sustain the service quality mini-loop of service standards, performance measurement, and rewards.

Service standards without measurement, or measurement without consequences, will capture no one's imagination. People at work need to know (1) what it is they are supposed to do,

(2) that they will be measured on how well they do it, and (3) that how they do will matter.

Closing the service quality mini-loop is essential to building a service-minded culture. From overbearing customers to boring, repetitive work to conflicting role definitions to restrictive policies and procedures, much can get in the way of service excellence. It is only when an organization's leaders tap deeply into the human spirit and challenge and inspire human beings to maximum achievement that it is possible to overcome all of the pitfalls and obstacles. To do this, service leaders have to use every possible tool, including the service quality mini-loop.

NOTES

1. Schein, Edgar H., *Organizational Culture and Leadership,* San Francisco: Jossey-Bass Inc., 1985, pp. 233–234.
2. Berry, Leonard L., Futrell, Charles M., and Bowers, Michael R. *Bankers Who Sell,* Homewood, IL: Dow Jones-Irwin, 1985, Chapter 5.
3. Gross, Laura, and Rosenstein, Jay. "Quality Service Standards Get New Attention." *Banking Week,* October 5, 1987, p. 22.
4. Zeithaml, Valarie A., Berry, Leonard L., and Parasuraman, A. "Communication and Control Processes in the Delivery of Service Quality." *Journal of Marketing,* April 1988, pp. 42–43.
5. Ibid., p. 43.
6. Larkin, Raymond J. "The History of Quality at American Express." *FYI,* October 9, 1987, pp. 2–3.
7. Berry, Leonard L., Futrell, Charles M., and Bowers, Michael R. *Bankers Who Sell.* Homewood, IL: Dow Jones-Irwin, 1985, p. 120.
8. "First Union's Service Guarantee." *Southern Banker,* December 1987.
9. Berry, Leonard L., Futrell, Charles M., and Bowers, Michael R. *Bankers Who Sell,* Homewood, IL: Dow Jones-Irwin, 1985, p. 127.
10. Peters, Tom. *Thriving on Chaos.* New York: Alfred A. Knopf, 1987.
11. Berry, Leonard L., and Rieder, George A. "Parade Is Festive Way to Honor Service Workers." *American Banker,* December 31, 1987.

CHAPTER 10

SERVICE QUALITY: A JOURNEY, NOT A DESTINATION

Service quality is a profit strategy, and I can prove it.
—*Willis Rhodes, Executive Vice President of
Operations and Information Systems,
First American National Bank, Nashville*

• A guest at the Holiday Inn on Union Square in San Francisco is trying to turn on his radio. No matter which button he turns—or which way he turns it—the radio will not work. After 15 minutes, the guest calls housekeeping to complain about a defective radio. Ten minutes later, a hotel employee delivers a brand new radio (still in plastic wrapper), a box of chocolates, and a red rose. As for the radio already in the room, the employee turns it on instantly (it plays perfectly) and then quickly reassures the guest that the radio is "tricky" to turn on. The employee pleasantly exits the room, leaving behind both radios, the chocolates, and the rose.

• An elderly woman is standing in the aisle of her favorite food store, Ukrop's Super Markets of Richmond, Virginia. She picks up a large pineapple from the display case, holds it for several moments, then reluctantly returns it. Ukrop's president, James Ukrop, sees the woman put back the pineapple and asks her if she would like the pineapple cut in half so she could buy one of the halves. She answers affirmatively and then explains that she lives alone and looks forward to coming to Ukrop's because the people are so friendly and she feels "welcome." Ukrop's fixes customers' flat tires in the parking lot, cleans customers' car windshields on snow days, and goes across

188

the street to a rival supermarket to buy out-of-stock items requested by customers. It is no mystery why Ukrop's, highly successful with 19 stores, has earned a reputation among Richmond food shoppers for legendary service.

• A customer is trying on a slacks and blouse outfit in a Palais Royal dressing room. It is soon apparent that the outfit is not going to work. The slacks are too tight and the appeal of the blouse is that it goes with the slacks. What to do? In most stores, the customer would have to put back on her own clothing and leave the dressing room to find the salesperson. But this is Palais Royal, a successful 28-store Houston chain, and the customer needs only to push the dressing room call button to summon the salesperson. Actually, the salesperson may already be outside the dressing room as Palais Royal's culture is "to beat the bell."

• Flying home from Maui after staying in an elegant new Marriott hotel over Christmas, a traveler finds herself sitting next to Marriott CEO Bill Marriott. Mr. Marriott asks the traveler for her reaction to the hotel. The traveler speaks not of luxurious and beautiful facilities, but of a hotel staff that cared enough to hang a Christmas stocking full of cookies and other goodies on her room doorknob, Christmas day. The passenger raves about how good the Christmas stocking made her feel on a lonely day when she wanted to be with her family.

Beginning this final chapter with these stories reminds us at the outset that the essence of services marketing is service.The textbooks stress the four Ps of marketing—product, place, promotion, and price—but in a service business, marketing directors have the most at stake with a fifth "P," which is performance.[1]

A financial institution is a service business; it markets performances, not things. What kind of future can a financial institution have if its service is poor? What kind of opportunity can it have to compete, to solidify customer relationships, to grow? Financial services competition is on a rampage; every day new competitors enter the financial services business. To what can a financial institution turn to differentiate itself, to build a distinct and compelling and sustainable image, if not service?

A low-price strategy is not the answer for most institutions because price is the most easily imitated element of the marketing mix. And how low can the price really go? Giving services away is no way to build a business.

Advertising is certainly important, but advertising is only worth investing in if the picture it paints is true. To promote an institution with deficient service is akin to inviting people to a bad party. The people may come to the party, but they don't stay long and they are less likely to respond to the next invitation.

Service excellence is the one competitive alternative open to financial institutions that is both important to customers and difficult for competitors to duplicate. We wrote this book because we consider the improvement of service to be the single most important competitive opportunity available to financial institutions. We consider quality service to be the very best antidote for intense competition. When too many financial service companies chase too few customers, it is the firms with mediocre and poor service that get hurt. The outstanding institutions, the Friendly Banks and University National Banks of the world, compete on the basis of service excellence and continue to grow and make money.

Quality service is a relationship builder; it is the surest way to create "true" customers who are glad to be doing business with the institution, who perceive the institution to be special, who praise the institution to others. Quality service drives market share.

Quality service also lowers the costs of doing business. Although quality initiatives typically involve some level of financial investment, the returns can pay off richly in improved productivity, higher employee morale and retention, fewer mistakes involving the costly reperformance of services, lower marketing costs, and higher prices.

With service excellence, there are no losers, only winners. Customers win. Employees win. Management wins. Stockholders win. Communities win. Delivering first-rate service is a profit strategy *for* everyone.

A RESPONSE TO THE COUNCIL ON
FINANCIAL COMPETITION

Not everyone agrees that service quality is a primary profit strategy for financial institutions. In October 1987, the Council on Financial Competition, Washington, D.C., issued a report in which it proposed that "Service quality as an issue is seriously overrated; service certainly is not as important as the mythic proportions it has taken on in industry trade publications and conferences."[2]

We believe this and other propositions in the Council's report are completely wrong. The Council's "overrated" proposition is in fundamental conflict with the purposes of this book, to communicate a sense of urgency for financial service quality and guide financial institution executives in taking the service quality journey. We will let the book as a whole "answer" the Council's report.

The Council defends the "overrated" proposition by citing a 1987 *American Banker* survey in which 92 percent of the consumer sample rated their banking service to be "good" or "excellent." The Council also concludes that, on average, only 10 to 15 percent of closed accounts can be attributed to service deficiencies.[3]

There are several problems with the Council's reasoning. For one thing, we do not know how many *American Banker* survey respondents who gave a good or excellent rating to their present financial institution(s) have, in fact, left other institutions because of poor service. In a 1987 national study of financial institution customers conducted by Raddon Financial Group for the Financial Institutions Marketing Association (FIMA), 42 percent of the sample indicated that they have changed financial institutions because of service problems. Younger consumers (aged 18 to 44 years) and those with higher incomes ($50,000 and above) were most likely to have switched. The average deposit balance of switchers was $23,000.[4]

A second point is that in the *American Banker* survey, the vast majority of good/excellent ratings were "good" (approximately 70 percent of the banking sample) rather than "excellent" (about 20 percent of the banking sample). Given the growing intensity of deregulated financial services competition, the question we ask is: "Is good good enough?"

A third point is that customer ratings of financial institutions reported in the survey may, in fact, be overstated—at least in some markets. In a 1987 study in California cited in the Council report, shoppers rated 41 percent of 3,658 visits to bank and thrift institution offices to be "fair" or "poor."[5]

A fourth point is that the figure the Council cites for service-related account closings (10 to 15 percent) is not a comforting figure. It may also be too low. Indeed, 1987 *American Banker* data indicate that among the 10 percent of the customers who moved their principal financial business to a new institution in the previous year, 21 percent did so because of service problems. Only a change of residence caused more people (25 percent) to move their financial business.[6] Whatever the service-instigated customer turnover rate is for a given financial institution, be it 10, 20, or 30 percent, it still represents many customers who are unnecessarily walking out the back door and who may be telling others not to enter the front door as well.

It is clear that we emphatically disagree with the Council's conclusion that quality as an issue in financial services is "seriously overrated." By the Council's own admission, its views in the report are "contrarian." In our opinion, the Council's views are also wrong.

SUMMING UP

We have used the "journey" metaphor to communicate the central idea that the pursuit of quality is an unending process. We have made the point, again and again, that service quality is not a "program." Quality is a function of culture, and culture is dynamic, not static. The levers of culture must be pushed continually. To not go forward is to go backward.

In these pages, we have presented many ideas, ideas that an institution's executives could discuss, debate, tailor, and mold into a plan for moving forward on service quality. As we near the end of the book, we summarize a selection of these ideas—first to reinforce them, but also to demonstrate that service quality is not the elusive, amorphous, impossible-to-grab-hold-of issue that it is sometimes thought to be.

1. *Service is what the customer says it is.* The customer's assessment of service quality is the only assessment that matters. Customers assess the service quality of an institution by evaluating the service they receive (perceptions) from the perspective of the service they desire (expectations). Institutions earn reputations for good service by consistently meeting or exceeding customer service expectations. These expectations can be categorized into five overall dimensions of service performance: looking good (tangibles); keeping the service promise (reliability); making the service accessible (responsiveness); providing knowledgeable and courteous service (assurance); and making a commitment to understanding and satisfying the customer (empathy).

2. *Improving service involves closing gaps.* To close the negative gap between what customers expect from the service and what they perceive they get requires closing other potential gaps—the gap between what customers expect and what management thinks they expect; the gap between what management thinks customers expect and the service specifications set for the organization; the gap between the service specifications and the service actually delivered; and the gap between the service actually delivered and what is said about the service in external communications.

3. *Quality is everybody's job.* In a financial institution, everyone has a customer. Customer service representatives. Auditors. Telephone receptionists. Proof operators. Tellers. Commercial lenders. Credit analysts. Marketing department personnel. Staff counsel. Secretaries. Guards. Everyone performs some type of service for someone else. Some have external customers, others have internal customers, but all have customers to serve. The opportunity for service excellence in an organization is greatest when individual employees assume responsibility for satisfying the service expectations of their customers.

4. *Quality is little things, not just big things.* Service excel-

lence is a matter of doing 101 little things better—"small winds" as one banker put it—not just doing a few big things well. When strategic parity reigns among competitors, little things often provide the competitive edge—a spotless service environment, a genuinely warm greeting from a service provider, a graceful handling of a special request, or a simple kindness that fits the moment like a glove. The great service companies use details to be different. They do things like install call buttons in dressing rooms or cut large pineapples in half for people who live alone. The great companies "major in minors."

5. *Good selling is part of good service.* Salespeople who help customers find just the right services to satisfy their particular requirements are providing good service. Few issues are more consequential or complex for individual households or organizations than issues of financial management. Financial institution salespeople who are professional and knowledgeable, who listen well and then come up with answers, and who stand by their customers after the sales are made are "servers." Sales and service are inseparable.

6. *The foundation for service excellence is culture.* Culture is the invisible yet powerful code of conduct that exists in organizations. Culture defines the "rules of the game," the essentials of "winning" behavior. Cultural change can be as much an act of "undoing" as "creating." If an organization's existing culture is uncongenial to matters of service excellence, if the emphasis is on saving money rather than serving customers, doing what is convenient rather than being convenient, or emphasizing the sale but not the service to support it, then a cultural barrier—a "service wall"—exists that must be broken down to make way for new ideas.

7. *"Managing" is not enough.* Service work can be hard and discouraging. It can be "numbing." Only genuine leadership at all levels of the organization can provide the inspiration necessary to sustain committed servers. People who serve need to work for people who have a vision worthy of embrace; who communicate that vision by deeds, not just words; who seek to transform what exists into something better; and who have a sense of urgency about running a first-rate operation. Only true leaders inspire others to be the best they can be, to go for excellence rather than fall prey to the temptations of mediocrity. "Managing" is not enough when the quest is service excellence.

8. *Middle managers are key figures in the service chain.* Top management works *through* middle managers, and front-line service providers work *for* middle managers. Middle managers, as their label suggests, are in the middle of everything. Top management may want service excellence, but middle managers are in the best position to observe, coach, cajole, challenge, and inspire service providers on a daily basis. Middle managers must be "middle leaders." Middle managers are a crucial internal target market for quality improvement initiatives. If middle managers are not on the service quality bus, the bus will break down.

9. *Success breeds success.* One of the surest ways to get the attention of service nonbelievers is by example. Pilot projects in selected organizational units—what we call in Chapter 5 "lighthouses for change"—can be used to demonstrate the payoffs of improved quality. The key is to select pilot projects that have the most promise for meaningful change. The service quality journey is never without mishaps and failures, but it is important to start with some heady success. As one banker puts it, "You better make damn sure that the first thing you try to invoke is successful and the benefits are clear."

10. *Service improvement efforts need to be anchored empirically.* Intuition, assumption, and personal experience are an insufficient basis for quality improvement efforts. The only way to really know what customers are thinking—what they expect from the service and what they perceive they are getting—is to ask them. Formal research with customers and noncustomers will reveal the dimensions of service performance that are most salient to target markets and least satisfactorily handled by the institution.

Service quality research should not stop with external customers and prospects. Equally important is research with employees, who are themselves customers of internal services and who know better than anyone else what is getting in the way of the services they perform.

Users of the service can tell the researcher what is happening. Providers of the service can explain why. Solid ongoing research with both groups provides the *only* basis for setting the service quality agenda—the sequence of action steps that are most needed to effect service quality improvement.

11. *Reliability and problem resolution make a powerful combination.* Customers expect service providers to be dependable and accurate. Reliability is the single most important dimension of service performance. Thus, even though "zero defects" is unlikely in the literal sense, it is important to push for this goal in the organization and to value it. A reliability rate of 97 percent may sound good, but what it really means is that 3 percent of an institution's hard-earned customers are not receiving the service they were promised; it also means, for a large institution with many customers and transactions, a lot of errors to correct.

The other half of the equation is being proactive in identifying those problems that do occur and being prepared to solve them. Customers are so used to experiencing additional problems when they attempt to resolve service problems that they are likely to be impressed when they experience quick, competent, and courteous problem resolution. The Holiday Inn radio story with which we started this chapter is an excellent example of exceeding the customer's expectations through effective problem resolution. The keys are encouraging customers to complain when they have problems, making it easy for them to do so, and then applying a sense of urgency, some creativity, and some grace in solving the problems. When all these keys are present, so is the opportunity to actually exceed the customers' expectations, to "bowl them over," to cement loyalties, and to fuel the word-of-mouth machine.

12. *The building of a service culture is boosted by a "service driver."* Effecting cultural change in an organization can be a full-time job, and senior management can benefit from the assistance of a service driver. Working closely with top management, the service driver instigates, coordinates, and supervises service-improving actions; identifies and supports cultural change agents throughout the organization; stimulates interorganizational communication and teamwork; shares expertises and solves problems; carries top management's message to service providers; and provides feedback from the field to top management. The ideal service driver has the ear of top management, broad operational experience, credibility in the organization, and the skill and knowledge to "get things done."

13. *Institutions need to organize for cultural change.* What is needed is a structural arrangement that provides broad interorganizational involvement in the change process itself and that accommodates change by offering a mechanism for evaluating and implementing ideas. A service quality steering group that includes members from various functional areas in the organization can be immensely helpful. Such a group can serve as a clearinghouse for ideas, recommend specific activities to upper management, and monitor progress. Members of the group also can help carry the service quality message to their own work units. More focused service quality groups within specific areas of the organization can spread involvement further and, if listened to, can pay off richly.

14. *Staffing starts with the customer.* Service providers need to be both willing and able to meet customer expectations. Accordingly, it is essential to recruit personnel who have the potential to do this, who have the background, intelligence, ability, desire and personality to be excellent service providers. This requires fresh thinking in financial institutions about hiring criteria, recruiting methods, compensation packages, career pathing, and related issues. Service is—and will always be—a human enterprise. Input shapes output. Seriously pursuing service quality involves taking staffing seriously—and always asking the question: "What kind of people do customers want serving them?"

15. *Service quality requires empowering service workers.* Service providers need room to maneuver. Leveraging the "freedom factor" for individual service providers—giving them the opportunity to "create" for their customers, to implement just the right solution for their customers—is an important thing to do. How can we expect service providers to be enthusiastic about a service role that allows them no room for judgment, that stifles their creativity, and that turns off their customers because of inflexibility of service? The answer is: "We can't."

Thick "rule books" do not pave the way to excellent service. What paves the way is building a strong service-minded culture, hiring outstanding people, preparing them to perform excellently in the service role, giving them a sense of owner- ship in the service quality mandate—and then getting out of their way so they can serve! Financial institution executives need to work hard at paring the rule book down to the true es- sentials and then letting the cultural "rules" guide behavior.

16. *Technology is important, too.* To think of quality service only in the context of personal service is a real mistake. The ATM network with excellent locations, excellent security arrangements, and excellent reliability contributes to excellent service. The computerized customer information system that instantaneously provides relevant data to a salesperson help- ing a customer put together a service package contributes to excellent service. The on-line computer system that allows a corporate comptroller to call up account balances and other fi- nancial data on an in-office CRT contributes to excellent ser- vice.

The smart application of technology can speed up service delivery, increase reliability, and liberate service providers from tasks more suited for machines than human beings. What is essential is to think of technology as a means to an end, not as an end in itself, and to design it explicitly to serve internal and external customers within the framework of strategy.

17. *Quality is a design issue.* Service quality must be a forethought, not an afterthought. It must be a way of thinking that influences each step in the development of new services, new policies, new technologies, and new facilities. Designing quality into new offerings instead of "force-fitting" quality ini- tiatives *after the fact* results in higher reliability for customers, higher morale for employees, and higher productivity for the organization.

Inattention to user requirements and carelessness with details are, regrettably, all too common in the design of new offerings. A service is a process, and it is necessary to design quality into the process. Customer-minded executives cannot afford to stay on the sidelines as services and support infra- structures are designed, leaving it to the "technical people" to do their thing. Design flaws can bedevil quality for a long, long time.

18. *Preparing people to serve involves more than training.* Skill training is both critical and insufficient in the pursuit of service excellence. Service providers need knowledge as well as skills. They need to be able to answer "what" and "why" questions to properly perform the service role; job-specific skills are not enough. Combining education with training can be a value-shaper, a confidence-builder, a motivator. Human beings need to "know" in order to "do."

19. *Skill and knowledge development is never-ending.* Skill and knowledge development should not be viewed in terms of "events." Yes, people participate in three-day workshops and one-week skill-building classes—events, to be sure. This is not the problem. The problem is when we send people to these events and then assume they are "trained and educated." Skill- and knowledge-building is an unending "flow"—people either progress or fall behind. The environment within and outside the organization keeps changing—new strategies, new technologies, new knowledge—and individual employees must keep up for the sake of their own competency, promotability, and self-esteem, and for the sake of the organization's collective service capability.

The best way to transform skill and knowledge development into an ongoing process is to emphasize multiple concepts— classroom, one-on-one and self-learning, centralized and decentralized learning, and learning by observing and "doing" as well as by listening and reading. Using multiple approaches plus incorporating service quality concepts into *all* training and education efforts in the institution encourages a skill and knowledge development "process."

20. *Skill and knowledge development is not a "pill."* Not all service deficiencies are correctible through training and education. Sometimes service problems are rooted in ill-conceived job definitions, inadequate performance standards, the lack of time or tools needed to do a job, or simply a mismatch between person and position. Skill and knowledge development is a potent, absolutely essential tool in the service quality journey, but it does not stand alone and it is not a cure-all.

21. *The service quality "mini-loop" is at the heart of the* *culture-building process.* Service quality is just "talk" until management establishes service standards based on customer expectations, measures service performance down to the individual employee level, and rewards those who perform excellently. When management closes the service quality mini-loop, it sends a strong message that service quality matters and that service quality is important enough to set standards for it, measure it, and reward it. Closing the service quality mini-loop gives the service journey a sense of credibility, realness, and tangibility that is not possible in its absence.

22. *Recognition drives the human engine.* What financial rewards, career advancement, and "pats on the back" all have in common is recognition for a job well done. The "psychology" of rewards is powerful stuff. More money is but one way to recognize superior performance. How management rewards performance, how it celebrates achievement, can be even more important—even more motivating—than the size of the reward itself. Recognition is the behavior of "noticing" and saying "thank you;" it comes in many effective forms.

WHAT IF YOUR BOSS IS A SERVICE SKEPTIC?

If we were to isolate one primary point of this book—one aspect of the service quality journey that stands above all others as an essential ingredient for success—it would be the personal commitment, support, and leadership of senior management. Only senior management can set in motion the sequence of decisions, actions, and events necessary to put the organization on the road to service quality and keep it there, from authorizing institution-wide research into customers' service expectations and perceptions, through measuring and rewarding service performance based on what customers expect "quality" service to be.

What happens, then, if the CEO, president, or other key decision-makers are *not* believers? What if the service skeptic is your boss? That particular roadblock is formidable indeed, but all is not lost. Granted, this situation carries with it a higher than average degree of risk, which is true whenever a manager is committed to a course of action not supported by his or her superiors. Timid managers, no matter how firm their convictions, are likely to keep their heads down, bide their time, and hope. More aggressive managers, however, will recognize that service quality is a watershed issue not just for the organization, but for the financial services industry as a whole —one of those rare waves that is likely to sweep nonbelievers away. As such, service quality as an issue has great potential as a "career-maker." Taking action may well be worth the personal risk.

Strategy One: Sell Your Boss

The first and most obvious strategy is to deal with the situation head-on and try to sell the boss on the importance of service quality. One possibility is to build a consensus on the importance of the service quality issue among the people who report directly to the boss. Few managers, faced with general agreement among their subordinates that a particular course of action is strategically critical to the business, will obstruct those efforts, provided there is no conflict with the organization's basic mission. We can think of no situation where building a service culture would be antithetical to other key organizational objectives.

If support can be developed among peers, the group can then band together to market the quality concept to the boss. In addition, it may be advantageous to bring in one or more credible outsiders—"expert witnesses"—who can lead internal seminars and make the case for quality. Taking the boss along to a well-chosen outside conference or two can also be helpful, as can selected reading material.

Strategy Two: Isolate and Contain Your Boss

A second strategy, assuming that the first one fails, is to isolate and contain the boss. This option is riskier, and usually involves approaching the boss's peers or superiors to test the waters on the service quality issue. In one institution we have worked with, the president was highly analytic and not particularly people-oriented. The service quality "champions" in this case were the heads of the bank's operations, marketing, and retail organization. Through informal means, they ascertained the interest of the chairman and CEO, and together obtained his support. The president, in turn, went along with the consensus opinion. And it was all done skillfully enough that the president didn't feel manipulated.

In effect, strategy two involves selling the boss's superiors or peers on service quality and then counting on them to sell the boss. The boss may become more interested if others in the power structure take a more active posture on the issue.

Strategy Three: Grafting

A third possibility is "grafting" a service quality focus onto another objective that has the unambiguous support of management—an aggressive expense reduction campaign, for example. The argument here would be that quality service is an important component of reducing rework and, consequently, reducing staff. Cutting staffing levels alone will not provide as great a return as reducing both staff and error rates.

Major strategic priorities of the organization can be examined to see which ones offer logical service quality tie-ins. By linking service quality to another initiative, the service quality champion who is otherwise obstructed has a chance of keeping the service quality issue alive until it earns enough visibility to stand unassisted.

Strategy Four: The Micro Approach

Still another option available to a service champion is to focus all energies on improving service quality within the part of the organization he or she manages—a single operating unit, region, or group of branches. With this strategy, it is usually best to keep a low profile in the early stages, collecting baseline data to help build a case later for why service quality initiatives should be broadened.

Success gets people's attention. In most organizations,

other operating unit heads will start asking: "What is he doing to improve returns?" or "Why are her people happier and more productive?" Word will get around. When the time is right, the service message can be carried high into the organization, above the obstructing manager.

QUICK FIXES DO NOT EXIST

This book contains no magical answers to the service quality question. Materially improving service requires determined, unrelenting, inspired, knowing leadership at the top of an organization and throughout its nooks and crannies. It also takes time. There are no "quick fixes," no overnight solutions, no simple formulas.

The service quality job is never done; the only real options are to be proactive and try to get better or to ignore the quality issue and hope for the best. The proactive option calls for a "game plan"—a melding of ideas and action steps, structural arrangements and systems, people and machines—that fits a specific organization at a specific point in time. We have discussed the key concepts in this book; it is up to you to take it from here.

It won't be easy, of course, At times, it may seem like you are spinning your wheels, moving around the same circle like a hamster in a cage. But improving service in a service business is a *smart* thing to do, and if you take a thoughtful approach to the challenge, rally others to help, and think in terms of "evolution" rather than "revolution," you will eventually see some movement, some progress. And then—if you keep the pressure on and don't get complacent—you will start to see success feeding success, movement turning to momentum.

Service quality is a powerful profit strategy for financial institutions. It is also more fun. Most of us want to work in an "achievement culture." We want to be part of a genuine team effort. We want to do good!

So we say to you: "Go for it. Assume a mantle of service leadership." As Rabbi Hillel said hundreds of years ago, "If not me, who? If not now, when?"

NOTES

1. Berry, Leonard L. "In Services, Little Things Make the Big Stories." *American Banker,* April 28, 1988.
2. *Service Quality.* Washington, D.C.: Council on Financial Competition, October 1987, p. 3.
3. Ibid.
4. *Financial Institutions Marketing Association Strategic Research and Planning Program—An Ongoing Study of Marketing Strategies for Savings Institutions.* Raddon Financial Group, Spring 1987, p. 132.
5. *Service Quality.* Washington, D.C.: Council on Financial Competition, October 1987, p. 22.
6. Gross, Laura. "Elite Customers Move the Most, Account-Switching Study Shows." *American Banker,* October 5, 1987.

INDEX